5/2015

A Beaded
Romance

Kelly Wiese

26 BEADWEAVING PATTERNS
AND PROJECTS FOR
GORGEOUS JEWELRY

D&C
David and Charles

Contents

Introduction   4

Beadweaving Basics   6

Tools and Materials   8
Basic Stitches and Techniques   10
Circle stitch   10
Backstitch   11
Chevron stitch   13
Double spiral rope   14
Flat herringbone   15
Flat round herringbone   16
Flat round peyote   17
Odd-count tubular peyote   18
Right-angle weave   19
St. Petersburg chain   20
Tubular picot netting   21

Projects   22

Victorian Circles Necklace and Bracelet   24
Picot Petals Pendant and Ring   32
Sequins in Symmetry Bracelet and Earrings   39
Midnight Lace Necklace   44
Drop Anklet   49
Fringed Pendant and Bracelet   52
Crystal Flower Necklace   62
Mobile Necklace and Earrings   68
Rivoli Flowers Bracelet   75
Ruffled Rings Necklace   80
Flower Garland Necklace and Bracelet   84
Cameo Necklace   91
Beadazzled Necklace and Bracelet   96
Regency Necklace   107
Ribbon Lace Necklace and Bracelet   114
Circular Paths Necklace and Earrings   124
Coming Up Roses Lariat   135

Index   140
About the Author   142

Introduction

Beading is my passion, but books are not far behind, so being able to have my name on a beading book was a dream come true. Being able to do a second book has been just as rewarding as doing my first book, *Beaded Allure*. I've learned more lessons along the way, one of which is to make more notes so I can remember what I did previously. Then I just have to remember where I put the notes!

With this book, I wanted to offer my fellow beaders more romantic, delicate designs to choose from. Over time my style has evolved, but one thing has stayed relatively the same: my love of designing jewelry that tends to be a little on the vintage side but with a modern edge.

My color choices are often subtle. I love jewel tones and metallics and use them in most of my work. I do encourage you to discover and follow your own color preferences. In the book's projects, I refer to "main" colors and "accent" colors; the colors of beads you select for these is entirely up to you. (Within parentheses following the bead types in each materials list are the bead colors I used for the projects shown.)

These designs are a jumping-off point. They can be made as is, or they can be adapted and changed to suit your own tastes. Explore all the possibilities that you can dream of.

I have had some fantastic opportunities over the last several years, and I have met some amazing people. Since my first book came out, my world has expanded and it has been a great experience. The love and support that exists in the beading community is marvelous, and I am very happy to be a part of it.

If you are a new beader, I encourage you to enter the wonderful world of beading. This book will give you some basic skills and help you to build upon them. If you are an experienced beader, I think you will find inspiring projects to pique your interest. Either way, I hope you enjoy using this book as much as I enjoyed creating the projects.

Beadweaving Basics

This section will cover some of the basic stitches used in the projects. Look them over and get a feel for them. It will also cover the items you need to get started. Thankfully, beadweaving doesn't require a lot of expensive tools and materials. Experiment with the different threads, needles and materials available until you find the ones that you like best. Ask any experienced beader and you will find that each one has favorites that are sworn by.

Tools and Materials

Thread

There are several different types of beading thread to choose from. I prefer **Nymo Size D** (Nymo comes in a variety of sizes). It is an inexpensive nylon thread that comes in a wide range of colors. Size D is fairly strong but thin enough to get several passes of thread easily through size 11 and size 15 Japanese seed beads.

FireLine is another option. It comes in several different weights and colors. It is great for working with crystals and other beads that have sharp edges, as it tends to be a little stronger than thread.

One-G is a thread from TOHO Beads out of Japan. It is a little more expensive than Nymo. It does come in a nice selection of colors. I have found it to be easy to work with.

Silamide is a twisted thread that is fairly strong. It also comes in several different colors.

Thread conditioners

Thread Heaven is an inexpensive, synthetic thread conditioner that lasts a very long time. I find that it helps to keep my thread from knotting, so I use it for all my projects.

Beeswax is a good option if you are making a vessel or a piece that needs more support. It can make your beadwork a little stiffer, but it can fill up the beads with wax. Use it sparingly so you don't clog up your beads!

There is also a **synthetic beeswax**. I like it better than natural beeswax because it doesn't fill up the beads as much and it's not as sticky.

Beading mats

When working with seed beads, it is always a good idea to have a soft surface to spread out your beads. I use the vellux bead mats that most bead stores carry.

They come in different colors and can be cleaned in the washer and dryer. Consider cutting up a vellux blanket to have lots of bead mats! **Ultrasuede** or **suede** also works nicely. Glue or tape a piece of vellux or suede into a **plastic tray** (a tray without a deep side works best) for a great surface to spread out your beads. The small lip helps to keep the beads from rolling off the material.

Needles

Needles come in a variety of sizes. I use **size 12 beading needles**. They are fairly long, and I find that they easily fit through seed beads with several passes of thread. They are also a little flexible, which can be an asset when you have a tight space to bead through.

A **size 11 beading needle** is slightly larger and has a larger eye. If you have a hard time threading the needle, this is a good size to use.

Some beaders like **sharp needles**. They are much shorter than a beading needle, but they come in the same sizes as beading needles. When working with suede for bead embroidery, they can be a useful option.

Task lamp

Good lighting is key to beadwork. A **full-color spectrum light**, such as an OttLite, imitates natural light. This type of light is ideal for picking out colors.

Other small desk lights also work, but it's best to avoid picking out colors under a yellow-hued light; picking out the colors in sunlight will give you better results.

Some lights also come with a **magnifier**, a useful accessory for any beader.

Pliers

It can be handy to have a small pair of pliers with smooth jaws. They can be used to break a bead to correct a mistake or to pull your thread through a bead that is getting full of thread (just be careful when you do this because you can end up breaking a bead you didn't want to break).

Beads

Japanese seed beads come in a variety of sizes. The larger the number, the smaller the bead. The projects in this book use mostly size 11 and size 15 seed beads. Sizes 6 and 8 seed beads make nice accent beads. Seed beads also come in many colors and finishes. I tend to stay away from galvanized beads and those that have dyed finishes because the color can rub off or fade.

Fire polish beads are glass beads that are fairly inexpensive. They are faceted and add a nice touch to beadwork. They are measured by the millimeter.

Nothing shines quite like true **crystal beads**! I use a lot of Swarovski **bicone crystals** in these projects. **Crystal rivolis** make great focal points. (Rivolis are crystal stones, not beads, because they are not drilled.)

Glass pearls are a great combination with seed beads. Swarovski makes them in a variety of sizes and shapes. **Czech glass pearls** also look nice and can be a more affordable option.

Druk beads are round Czech glass beads. They come in a variety of sizes measured by millimeter. I like to use druk beads as clasp beads.

Delica beads, made by Miyuki of Japan, are a uniform cylinder type of bead. They are great for working peyote because they fit together nicely.

Other

When starting a piece of bead embroidery, there is often a focal cabochon or crystal that needs to be adhered to a backing surface before you can start. I like to use a **medium to heavy interfacing** for my backing material for bead embroidery. Lacy's Stiff Stuff is another good option, especially for larger pieces, as it is thicker than interfacing. I use **Ultrasuede** for the final backing with bead embroidery. It is usually used with an edging row, and it is fairly easy to get a needle through.

E-6000 is my favorite adhesive to use for bead embroidery. It creates a good bond with the backing material and crystals and stone or glass cabochons.

Basic Stitches and Techniques

Techniques are the building blocks for all beadweaving. Learn a few basic stitches and you will be on your way to creating gorgeous jewelry.

Working with thread

The projects in this book require lots of thread, typically in varying lengths and performing multiple functions within a piece. Here are a few definitions and guidelines to follow while creating your jewelry.

Stop bead

When you begin a project, you may be instructed to add a stop bead. A **stop bead** is used to prevent the beads of the project from sliding off the end of the thread. This bead may or may not be worked into the project, so it helps to read the project instructions in advance to determine its use. To add a stop bead to the thread, refer to **Circle stitch** in the next column; the thread follows the same path in one bead, without adding any extra beads.

Working thread

The **working thread** has the needle on it. When starting a new thread in a piece, I like to leave about 6" (15cm) of the old thread (that now becomes a tail), then add the new thread.

To add the new thread, tie it onto the thread between the beads using **half-hitch knots**. To tie a half-hitch knot (see diagram), go under the thread that is between the bead your working thread is coming out of and the very next bead. Leave a small loop and then go through the loop from the top with the working thread. Pull the working thread tight and then go through the next bead. This hides the knot in between the beads. It is best to tie two or three half-hitch knots between the beads when tying off your tail ends.

HALF-HITCH KNOT

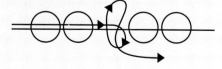

Tail thread

The **tail thread** is the thread hanging off the piece. Tail threads can have one of two fates: they will either be used to help complete a project, or they will be left until the end of the project to be woven into the beadwork.

At the end of every project, you'll be instructed to weave in all the tail threads. To do this, thread the needle onto a tail thread. Weave this thread into the beadwork away from the place it exits from, and tie a few half-hitch knots to secure it (you do not have to weave the entire length of the thread). You can snip off any remaining old thread.

Reinforcing

The instructions will often reference reinforcing the piece with either the tail thread or the working thread. To reinforce, weave the working thread through the beadwork, following the previous thread path. You may or may not be instructed to end the thread at this point. Reinforcing is almost always done at the clasp ends of bracelets and necklaces.

Circle stitch

A circle stitch looks just like it sounds—the thread path makes a circle (see photo). Circle stitching is used a lot in the projects because it's a great way to bring various elements together.

Backstitch for bead embroidery

Bead embroidery can be worked on any number of surfaces. The backstitch is used to sew beads onto a work surface. It is a good basic stitch for embellishing or for creating the base row to build a peyote bezel. A bezel is a beautiful way to incorporate a loose crystal or cabochon into a design by enclosing the edge tightly with beads. I like to use a medium to heavy interfacing (the kind without the iron-on fusing) as my work surface.

When sewing around a crystal or cabochon (instructions below), work in the direction that feels most comfortable.

Adhesive Tips for Bead Embroidery

• Always be sure to leave plenty of extra interfacing around the edges of your cabochon or crystal. You can always trim the extra off, but it is much harder to add if you don't start with a big enough piece.

• If you have a slightly pointed crystal, fold the piece of interfacing in half and then in half again. Snip a small piece off the folded corner to make a small diamond-shaped hole in the center of the interfacing. Then when you glue the crystal to the interfacing, the point can go through the small hole you created.

• Use a toothpick to spread a thin layer of glue onto the back of the crystal or cabochon. Then press the piece onto the interfacing. Wipe off any seeping glue. It doesn't take long for the glue to set enough for you to start beading.

BACKSTITCH FOR BEAD EMBROIDERY PATTERN

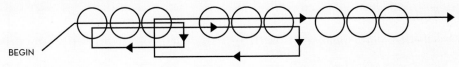

BEGIN

BACKSTITCH INSTRUCTIONS

Adhere the crystal or cabochon to the interfacing (see *Adhesive Tips for Bead Embroidery*).

Start a new thread and put a knot at the end that is large enough to hold in the interfacing. Beginning on the longer side of the crystal or cabochon rather than at a curve or point, bring the needle and thread up through the interfacing to the top side. It helps if you work at a slight angle so the stitches stay as close to the crystal as possible.

Pick up 3 beads, pull them down the thread and lay them alongside the crystal or cabochon. Sew down at the end of them. Come back up the interfacing at the beginning of the beads (where the knot is) and sew through all 3 beads again.

Pick up 3 beads, pull them down the thread to lay them along the crystal in line with the first 3 beads and sew down

at the end of them. Come back up between the beads and the crystal and go through the last bead in the previous group and the 3 beads just added. You are going through 4 beads at this point. (This connects the 3 beads just added with the previous 3 beads and results in the beads laying more evenly around the crystal.)

Continue working backstitch around the rest of the crystal or cabochon.

When you are finished stitching, bring the thread to the back of the piece. Tie the thread to secure it, and trim off any excess thread.

CHEVRON STITCH

DOUBLE SPIRAL ROPE

FLAT HERRINGBONE

FLAT ROUND HERRINGBONE

FLAT ROUND PEYOTE

ODD-COUNT TUBULAR PEYOTE

RIGHT-ANGLE WEAVE

ST. PETERSBURG CHAIN

TUBULAR PICOT NETTING

Chevron stitch

The chevron stitch works up quickly and can be done in a variety of widths. It looks great on its own or with embellishments added. It can be done in a single color or multiple colors for a new look. Different sizes of beads can also be used. For this example, I used two colors so the pattern is easier to follow. A chevron stitch is used on the **Mobile Necklace** (page 68) for the strap.

1 Pick up 1 main bead and go back through it from the tail end to turn it into a stop bead. Pick up 7 more main beads and 1 accent bead. Then go back through the first 4 main beads, including the stop bead.

2 Pick up 1 main bead, 1 accent bead and 4 main beads. Then skip over the next 2 main beads of the original circle and go through the next main bead of the original circle.

3 Pick up 1 main bead, 1 accent bead and 4 main beads. Then skip over the first 2 main beads from the group of 4 from the last row and go through the third main bead from the last row. Repeat until the chain is the desired length.

Double spiral rope

The double spiral is a good technique for beaded ropes. It makes a beautiful, substantial rope. Using different colors really brings out the pattern. The core beads are size-8 Japanese seed beads. These can get a little tight and hard to get through as the rope is worked. I sometimes use a straight pin to go down through the core beads to help separate them so that I can get the needle and thread through them. I used this rope on the **Regency Necklace** (page 107), but I also love to make bracelets with this pattern. It looks great all on its own.

1 Pick up 4 size-8 beads, 3 color #1 beads, 1 size-8 bead and 3 color #1 beads. Then go back through the first 4 size-8 beads just picked up.

2 Pick up 3 color #2 beads, 1 size-8 bead and 3 color #2 beads. Then go back through the original 4 size-8 beads. (The size-8 beads are the core of the spiral, and they will always be the beads you go back through.)

3 Pick up 1 size-8 bead, 3 color #1 beads, 1 size-8 bead and 3 color #1 beads. Then go back through the last 3 size-8 beads of the core, and also go back through the first size-8 bead just picked up. Then push the beads added over to the left.

4 Now flip the entire piece of beadwork over so that the color #2 beads are on the left side. Pick up 3 color #2 beads, 1 size-8 bead and 3 color #2 beads. Then go back through the last 4 size-8 core beads. Now flip the beadwork over again so that the color #1 beads are on the left.

Every time beads are added, they need to be added to the left side. Repeat the last 2 steps until the rope is the desired length.

Flat herringbone

Flat herringbone is used for making bracelet bands and necklace straps. It is a soft, supple stitch that can be worked in a variety of widths. I used flat herringbone for the **Coming Up Roses Lariat** (page 135).

There is more than one way to start flat herringbone; I think this method is a fairly easy way to start and work the stitch. Flat herringbone is worked with an even number of beads. The turnaround can also be done without adding the extra bead to the edge for a cleaner look.

1 Pick up 2 beads and go back through them from the tail end so that they sit side by side. Pick up 1 bead and go back through the last bead added on the opposite side from where the thread originally exited, and also go through the bead just picked up. Keep adding beads this way until there are 6 beads in a row.

2 Pick up 2 beads and go down the second bead of the first row and come up the third bead. Pick up 2 beads and go down the fourth bead of the first row and come up the fifth bead. Pick up 2 beads and go down the sixth bead of the first row. Pick up 1 bead and go up the second bead just added.

3 Pick up 2 beads and go down the next bead from the last row and up the next one. Repeat 2 more times. On the third stitch, after going down the last bead from the last row, pick up 1 bead and then go up the last bead just added for the turnaround. Repeat to the desired length.

Flat round herringbone

Flat round herringbone is a great stitch used on its own or as the basis for something like a bezel for a crystal rivoli. I used it in the **Sequins in Symmetry** patterns (page 39) and also for the **Flower Garland** patterns (page 84). The number of beads in the beginning circle can be adjusted for different sizes of circles. Like so many stitches, it can also be started in various ways. This is just one way.

1 Pick up 6 beads and then go through all 6 beads again from the tail end. Also go forward through the first bead again to tighten the circle. Pick up 1 bead and go forward through the next bead of the original circle of 6 beads. Repeat 5 more times. After adding the last bead, also go through the first bead added in the second row.

2 Pick up 2 beads and go through the next bead from the last row of 6 beads. Repeat 5 more times. After adding the last set of 2 beads, also go through the first bead of the first set of 2 beads added in this row.

3 Pick up 2 beads and then go down the next bead of the first set of 2 beads from the last row. Then go up the first bead of the next set of beads from the last row. Repeat 5 more times. After adding the last set of beads, go through the first bead of the first set of beads from the last row and also through the first bead of the first set of beads added in this row.

From this point, you can add beads between the stacks to create a larger circle as the rows are worked. Those beads can also be turned into additional stacks of beads as an increase to the herringbone—the possibilities are many.

Flat round peyote

Flat round peyote is another stitch that works well as a component on its own or used as a base for a bezel for a crystal rivoli. I like to start this stitch with three beads and build out from there, adding increases to make the circle larger. You can use different colors of beads or even different sizes of beads to make the circles. I used flat round peyote on the **Rivoli Flowers Bracelet** (page 75).

1 Pick up 3 beads and then go back through them again from the tail end. Also go forward through the first bead again.

2 Pick up 2 beads and go through the next bead from the previous row. Repeat 2 more times. There should be 6 beads in this row. After the last beads are added, also go through the first bead added in this row.

3 Pick up 1 bead and go through the next bead from the previous row. Repeat until there are 6 beads in this row. After the last bead is added, also go forward through the first bead added in this row.

4 Pick up 2 beads and go through the next bead from the previous row. Repeat for a total of 12 beads in this row. After the last beads are added, also go forward through the first bead added in this row.

5 Pick up 1 bead and go through the next bead from the previous row. Repeat for a total of 12 beads in this row.

Odd-count tubular peyote

Odd-count tubular peyote is another good technique for making ropes for necklaces. It can be worked with various numbers of beads for different rope thicknesses. It is a little time-consuming, but the resulting ropes are flexible and perfect for pendants. With odd-count tubular peyote, there is no step up for each row; it just spirals around. I used odd count tubular peyote for the **Picot Petals Pendant** (page 32).

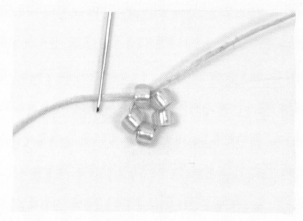 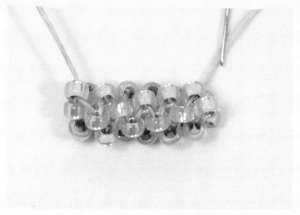

1 Pick up 5 beads and go back through them again from the tail end. Then, go forward through the first bead again to tighten the circle.

2 Pick up 1 bead, skip over the next bead and go through the next one. Repeat 1 more time. Then pick up 1 bead and go through the first bead added. The beads need to sit on top of each other.

Keep picking up 1 bead, skipping over the recessed bead and going through the next bead. The rope should start to spiral up. Pull snug. Repeat until the rope is the desired length.

Right-angle weave

Right-angle weave sometimes gets a bad rap for being hard to learn. However, it follows several basic thread paths and once you have those mastered, it is a piece of cake. It helps to think of the stitches or units as squares, with each square having a top, bottom and two sides. This applies no matter how many beads you are using to form the square's sides. I used right-angle weave variations in the **Fringed Pendant and Bracelet** (page 52), the **Beadazzled** set (page 96), and the **Circular Paths** set (page 124). Like peyote stitch, it is very versatile and well worth learning.

1 Pick up 4 beads and then go back through all 4 beads again from the tail end. Then, go through the first bead again to pull the beads closer together. Pick up 3 more beads and go back through the bead the thread originally exited from on the opposite side, and also go through the first 2 beads of the 3 just picked up. Pick up 3 beads and go back through the bead the thread originally exited from on the opposite side, and also go through the first bead of the 3 just picked up.

2 Pick up 3 beads and go back through the bead the thread originally exited from on the opposite side. Also go through the 3 beads just picked up and then go through the bead of the next square.

3 Pick up 2 beads and go through the side bead of the previous square, and then go through the bead the thread originally exited from on the opposite side. Also go through the first bead of the 2 just picked up.

4 Pick up 2 beads and go through the bottom bead of the next square of the previous row, and also go back through the bead the thread exited from on the opposite side. Also go through the first bead of the 2 just picked up. Repeat until the beadwork is the desired length.

St. Petersburg chain

This chain is easy and very pretty on its own or when combined with other stitches. Using two colors on the chain gives it a nice look, and the chain can also be made wider. I used the chain for the band of the **Drop Anklet** (page 49).

1 Pick up 4 beads and go back through the first and second bead from the tail end. Then pick up 1 more bead and go through the third and fourth bead of the original 4 beads. Pull snug.

2 Pick up 4 beads and go back through the first 2 beads just picked up. Pull snug and make sure that the beads are close to the previous group of beads.

3 Pick up 1 bead and go back through the 2 beads that the thread is coming out of on the same side, and also go through the next bead of the next group.

4 Pick up 1 bead and go through the 2 beads that are next to the 3 you just went through. Pull snug. Repeat until the chain is the desired length.

Tubular picot netting

Tubular picot netting is time-consuming but makes such a pretty rope. It has more of a lacy look than just regular tubular netting. I used tubular picot netting on the **Crystal Flower Necklace** (page 62).

1 Pick up 1 bead and turn it into a stop bead by going back through it from the tail end. Pick up 6 beads and then go back through the third bead of the 6 just picked up in a circular thread path. This will make a picot. Pull it snug against the other beads.

2 Pick up 6 beads and go through the third bead of the 6 just picked up to make another picot. Pull it snug against the other picot. Repeat one more time. Pick up 2 beads and then turn the beads into a circle by going through the first bead (the stop bead).

3 Now the beadwork will start to form a rope. Pick up 5 beads and go through the second bead just picked up to make a picot. Pick up 1 bead and then go through the tip bead of the next picot from the first row. Work in a circular thread path.

4 Repeat the previous step twice.

5 Keep adding picots following the last two steps until the rope is the desired length.

Projects

One of the wonderful features of beadweaving is that you can customize the projects to fit you. Color, size and aspects of any design can be altered to fit your vision. Some beaders prefer to re-create a piece exactly as designed, while others want to change it a little or a lot. It's all up to you.

I always encourage beaders at any skill level to read through all the instructions before starting a project. You might not understand everything until you start working through the steps, but you'll get a general idea of what is involved. Also, take a moment to double-check your bead count. For example, if your instructions say to pick up 28 beads for the first row, make sure that is what you have. Better to count twice than have to take apart once. It can also help to count out and group the beads needed for a row, especially if you're a beginner. When your grouping is gone, the row should be done. Just be sure to keep your counted beads away from curious kids and cats!

The rating system on these projects is a guideline to help the more inexperienced beader decide where to start. One-star projects are suitable for beginners to advanced beaders. These are good projects to start with. Two-star projects are for intermediate to advanced beaders. It helps to have a little beadweaving experience before you try these. Three-star projects are for advanced beaders. Don't start with these unless you are familiar with the stitches or techniques used or have some beadweaving experience.

Victorian Circles Necklace and Bracelet

When I first started designing, I didn't have a clear vision or style. I just made things that I liked. Over the years, my style emerged and most of my work tends to be feminine and delicate, sometimes with a Victorian look. This early design is no exception. It goes together rather quickly and is a good project for beginners.

 ○ ○ **DIFFICULTY LEVEL**

Necklace Materials

Size 12 beading needle

Size D Nymo beading thread or FireLine

(62) 4mm fire polish beads (Copper Luster)

(3) 9mm x 6mm smooth drop beads (Dark Bronze)

8mm round bead (Dark Bronze)

10 grams size-11 Japanese seed beads for main color (Metallic Dark Bronze)

3 grams size-11 Japanese seed beads for accent color (Lined Green)

Bracelet Materials

Size 12 beading needle

Size D Nymo beading thread or FireLine

(48) 4mm fire polish beads (Copper Luster)

8mm round bead (Dark Bronze)

6 grams size-11 Japanese seed beads for main color (Metallic Dark Bronze)

2 grams size-11 Japanese seed beads for accent color (Lined Green)

Necklace

Center circle pattern 1
Start with approximately 1 yard (.9m) of thread, single thickness with no knot. Pick up a main color bead and a 4mm bead. Repeat until there are a total of 10 of each bead. Then tie the beads into a circle. Leave a 4" to 6" (10cm to 15cm) tail. Weave forward through several beads and come out of one of the main color beads.

Center circle pattern 2
Pick up 3 main color beads, skip over the next 4mm bead and go through the next main color bead. Repeat until there is a set of 3 main color beads over each 4mm bead. After the last set of 3 beads are added, also go through the first 2 beads of the first set of 3 beads in this row.

Center circle pattern 3
Pick up 2 main color beads, an accent bead and 2 main color beads. Go through the center bead of the next set of 3 main color beads from the previous row. Repeat around the entire circle. After the last set of beads are added, also go through the first 3 beads of the first set of beads of this row. Weave the tail thread in and tie it off. Leave the working thread attached. Set this, the center circle of the necklace, aside for now.

Large circle
Make 2 more circles the same way as center circle pattern step 1. However, work the first row with 8 sets of beads instead of 10 sets. Then follow center circle pattern steps 2-3 to add the second and third row. Tie off the tail threads but leave the working threads attached on the 2 circles.

Medium circle
Make 5 more circles the same way as center circle pattern step 1. However, work the first row with 6 sets of beads instead of 10 sets. Then follow center circle pattern step 2 to add a set of 3 main color beads over each 4mm bead. Tie off the tail threads but leave the working threads attached.

Small circle
Make 1 circle the same way as the center circle pattern step 1. However, work the first row with 4 sets of beads instead of 10 sets. Then pick up 2 main color beads, 1 accent bead and 2 main color beads. Skip the next 4mm bead and go through the next main color bead. Repeat 3 more times. Tie off the tail thread but leave the working thread attached.

Assembly 1

Pick up the center circle and one of the 8-bead circles. The working thread on the center circle should be coming out of an accent bead of the last (third) row. Go through an accent bead on the third row of the 8-bead circle. Then go back through the accent bead of the center circle on the opposite side from where the thread originally exited. This is a circle stitch (see page 10). This is the primary stitch used to connect the circles.

Assembly 2

Weave over to the next accent bead of the center circle and circle stitch the corresponding accent bead of the 8-bead circle to the center circle. Tie off the working thread.

Assembly 3

Attach the other 8-bead circle to the other side of the center circle following assembly steps 1–2, using the working thread from the 8-bead circle. There should be 2 accent beads at the top of the center circle between the connections.

Assembly 4

Weave a working thread on a 6-bead circle so that it is coming out of a middle bead of the second row. Circle stitch it to the accent bead of the third row on one of the 8-bead circles. It should be the accent bead next to the center circle attachment.

Assembly 5

On the 6-bead circle, weave down to the middle bead of the third set of 3 beads from where it is attached to the 8-bead circle. Pick up 3 main color beads, 1 accent bead, 1 drop bead and 3 accent beads. Skip the 3 accent beads and go back up the drop bead, the accent bead and the 3 main color beads. Go through the middle bead of the circle on the opposite side from where the thread originally exited. Attach another 6-bead circle to the other 8-bead circle on the other side of the center circle, and then add a drop bead in the same way. Tie off the working thread.

Assembly 6

Pick up another 6-bead circle and weave the working thread so that it is coming out of the end bead of one of the groups of 3 main color beads. Pick up a main color bead, a 4mm bead and a main color bead. Go through the second accent bead of the center circle from where the attachment is to the 8-bead circle. Go back down the main color bead, the 4mm bead and the next main color bead. Go through the bead your thread originally exited from on the opposite side.

Assembly 7

Weave over to the next accent bead of the center circle and repeat assembly step 6 on the other end bead of the set of 3. Tie off the working thread.

Assembly 8

Weave the working thread on the 4-bead circle so that it is coming out of an accent bead on the second row. Circle stitch the accent bead to the middle bead of the third set of 3 beads of the 6-bead circle that was just attached.

Assembly 9
Weave down to the bottom accent bead of the 4-bead circle. Pick up 3 main color beads, 1 accent bead, 1 drop bead and 3 accent beads. Skip the 3 accent beads and go back up the drop bead, the accent bead and the 3 main color beads. Then go through the accent bead of the circle on the opposite side from where the thread originally exited. Tie off the working thread.

Assembly 10
Weave a working thread on another 6-bead circle so that it is coming out of the middle bead of one of the 3-bead sets on the second row. Circle stitch it to the third accent bead of the 8-bead circle. Repeat on the other side of the necklace with the last 6-bead circle. Leave the working threads attached.

Strap pattern
Weave the working thread on a 6-bead circle attached in assembly step 10 so that it is coming out of the middle bead of the third set of beads from where it is attached to the 8-bead circle. Pick up 6 main color beads, 1 accent bead and 6 main color beads. Go back through the middle bead of the circle on the opposite side from where the thread exited, and then back through the first 6 main color beads just picked up and the accent bead. Repeat, adding circles until the strap is the desired length. An average length is about 6½" (17cm) long and has 17 circles.

Closure pattern 1
After the strap is the desired length, the working thread should be coming out of the accent bead of the last circle. Pick up 6 main color beads, 1 accent bead, the 8mm bead and 3 accent beads. Skip the 3 accent beads and go back through the 8mm bead and the accent bead. Pick up 6 main color beads and go through the accent bead of the circle that the thread originally exited from on the opposite side. Reinforce.

Closure pattern 2
Repeat the strap pattern step on the other side of the necklace. End with the working thread coming out of the accent bead of the last circle. Pick up enough main color beads to fit comfortably but snugly around the 8mm bead. Go back through the accent bead the thread originally exited from on the opposite side. Reinforce. Tie off any remaining threads.

Bracelet

Bracelet pattern 1

Follow center circle pattern steps 1–3 and the large circle step of the necklace to make one 10-bead circle and two 8-bead circles. Then start a new thread approximately 1 yard (.9m) long, single thickness with no knot. Pick up a main color bead and a 4mm bead until you have a total of 6 of each bead. Tie the beads into a circle, leaving a 4" to 6" (10cm to 15cm) tail. Weave forward through the beads and come out of one of the main color beads. Pick up 3 main color beads, skip over the next 4mm bead and go through the next main color bead. Repeat until there is a set of 3 main color beads over each 4mm bead. After the last set of 3 beads are added, also go through the first 2 beads of the first set of 3 beads of this row.

Bracelet pattern 2

Pick up 2 main color beads, 1 accent bead and 2 main color beads. Then go through the center bead of the next set of 3 main color beads from the previous row. Repeat until you have gone all the way around the circle. Tie off the tail thread but leave the working thread attached.

Make 1 more circle this size. Then make two 4-bead circles following the small circle step of the necklace. There are a total of 7 circles on the bracelet.

Bracelet pattern 3

Follow assembly steps 1–2 of the necklace to connect the center circle to one of the 8-bead circles. Then attach the other 8-bead circle to the other side of the center circle the same way. There should be 3 accent beads of the center circle on each side of the connections.

Bracelet pattern 4

Use a working thread on a 6-bead circle and attach it to the 8-bead circle at the third accent bead over from where the 8-bead circle is attached to the 10-bead circle. Use a circle stitch to do this. Then weave over to the next accent beads and circle stitch them together. Repeat with the other 6-bead circle on the other side of the bracelet.

Bracelet pattern 5

Weave a working thread from one of the 6-bead circles so that it is coming out of the second main color bead after the second accent bead where the 6-bead circle is connected to the 8-bead circle. Pick up 2 main color beads, 1 of the 4mm beads and 1 main color bead. Go through an accent bead on one of the 4-bead circles. Then go back through the main color bead you just picked up, and also go back through the 4mm bead. Pick up 2 main color beads and go through the end main color bead of the next set of beads. Reinforce.

Add the other 4-bead circle to the other end of the bracelet the same way.

Closure pattern 1

Weave a working thread on a 4-bead circle so that it is coming out of the accent bead across from the connection to the 6-bead circle. Pick up 3 main color beads, the 8mm bead and 3 accent beads. Skip the accent beads and go back through the 8mm bead and 1 of the main color beads. Pick up 2 main color beads and go back through the accent bead of the circle on the opposite side from where the thread originally exited. Reinforce.

Closure pattern 2

On the other end of the bracelet, the working thread should be coming out of the accent bead across from the connection to the 6-bead circle. Pick up 8 main color beads, 1 accent bead, 8 main color beads, 1 accent bead, 8 main color beads and 4 accent beads. Skip the last 3 accent beads and go back through the first accent bead of the last 4 picked up. Pick up 8 main color beads and go through the next accent bead. Repeat one more time. Pick up 8 main color beads and go back through the accent bead of the circle the thread originally exited from on the opposite side. This makes a series of circles for the clasp bead and makes the bracelet adjustable. Reinforce. Tie off any remaining threads.

Picot Petals Pendant and Ring

When I designed this pendant, I made several in different monochromatic colorways. The lavender turned out to be my favorite. The design would work well with more dramatic colors also.

The large flower can be a bit floppy. To stiffen up the petals, brush a light coat of Future clear floor polish on the beadwork and let it dry. This will not hurt the beads and will help the flower hold its shape.

 **DIFFICULTY LEVEL**

Pendant Materials

Size 12 beading needle

Size D Nymo beading thread or FireLine

(25) 4mm bicone crystals (Tanzanite)

5mm bicone crystal (Tanzanite)

(3) 12mm rivoli crystals (Tanzanite)

9mm x 6mm briolette drop bead (Tanzanite)

6mm round crystal (Tanzanite)

10 grams size-15 Japanese seed beads for main color (Lavender Opal Gilt Lined)

2 grams size-15 Japanese seed beads for accent color (Lavender Blue Gold Luster)

Ring Materials

Size 12 beading needle

Size D Nymo beading thread or FireLine

(12) 4mm bicone crystals (Tanzanite)

12mm rivoli crystal (Tanzanite)

3 grams size-15 Japanese seed beads for main color (Lavender Opal Gilt Lined)

2 grams size-15 Japanese seed beads for accent color (Lavender Blue Gold Luster)

Pendant

Large flower 1

Start with approximately 2½ yards (2.3m) of thread, single thickness with no knot. Pick up 12 main color beads and go back through them all again from the tail end. Also go forward through the first bead again to pull the circle closer together. Leave a 4" to 6" (10cm to 15cm) tail.

Large flower 2

Pick up 3 main color beads, skip the next bead of the original circle and go through the next bead. Repeat until there are 6 points. After adding the last point, also go through the first 2 beads of the first point of this row. This lines up the working thread for the next row.

Large flower 3

Pick up 5 main color beads and go through the middle (second) bead of the next point from the last row. Repeat until there are 6 new points. After adding the last point, also go through the first 3 beads of the first point of this row.

Large flower 4

Pick up 7 main color beads and go through the middle (third) bead of the next point from the last row. Repeat until there are 6 new points. After adding the last point, also go through the first 4 beads of the first point of this row.

Large flower 5

Pick up 5 main color beads and go through the middle (fourth) bead of the next point from the last row. Pull snug. This row will start to pull in. Repeat until there are 6 new points. After adding the last point, also go through the first 3 beads of the first point of this row. Insert a 12mm rivoli into the beadwork and pull snug.

Large flower 6

Pick up 3 main color beads and go through the middle (third) bead of the next point from the last row. Repeat until you have added 6 new points (they won't look like points at this time because the netting is decreasing). After adding the last point, also go through the first 2 beads of the first point of this row.

Large flower 7

Pick up 3 accent beads and go back through the main color bead the thread originally exited from on the opposite side. This will form a picot. Weave over to the middle bead of the next point of the last row and repeat. Repeat for 6 picots total.

Large flower 8

Weave down to a middle (fourth) bead of the row of netting with 7 beads per point. Pick up 1 accent bead, a 4mm crystal and 1 accent bead. Go through the middle bead of the next point from the 7-beads-per-point row. Repeat until there are 6 of the 4mm crystals. After adding the last crystal, also go through the first accent bead and first 4mm crystal added in this row.

Large flower 9

Pick up 11 main color beads and go back through the crystal the thread originally exited from on the opposite side, and also go through the first 3 main color beads of the 11 just added. Pick up 3 accent beads and go back through the main color bead the thread originally exited from on the opposite side. This will create a picot.

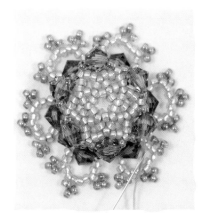

Large flower 10

Go through the next 3 main color beads. Pick up 3 accent beads and go back through the main color bead the thread originally exited from on the opposite side to create another picot. Repeat one more time. There should be 3 picots on the 11 main color beads.

Large flower 11

Weave over to the next 4mm crystal and repeat. Repeat until there is a loop with 3 picots around each 4mm crystal. This is the top layer of the large flower.

Large flower 12

Note: In this photo the beadwork is shown from the back. Weave down to a middle (third) bead of the first row of netting with 5 beads per point. Pick up 1 accent bead, a 4mm crystal and 1 accent bead. Go through the middle bead of the next point with 5 beads. Repeat until there are 6 of the 4mm crystals. After adding the last crystal, also go through the first accent bead and the first crystal added in this row.

Large flower 13

Pick up 14 main color beads and go back through the crystal the thread originally exited from on the opposite side. Also go through the first 3 beads of the 14 beads. Pick up 3 accent beads and go back through the main color bead the thread originally exited from on the opposite side. This makes a picot. Go through the next 3 main color beads and repeat. Repeat until there are a total of 4 picots on the loop of 14 main color beads.

Large flower 14

Weave over to the next crystal and repeat. Keep repeating until there is a total of 6 loops around the crystals with 4 picots on each loop.

Large flower 15

Weave the working thread so that it is coming out of a second bead on the row of netting with 7 beads per point. This will be between the layers of petals. Pick up 20 main color beads and go back through the main color bead the thread originally exited from on the opposite side. Reinforce several times. Repeat on the sixth bead of the same row. This makes a double bail for the rope strap. Tie off the tail and working thread. This completes the large flower.

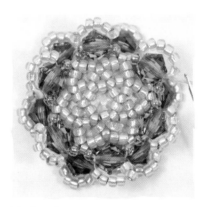

Medium flower 1

Start a new thread approximately 2 yards (1.8m) long, single thickness with no knot. Repeat large flower steps 1–8. Then pick up 6 main color beads and go back through the crystal the thread originally exited from on the opposite side. Weave over to the next crystal and repeat. Repeat until you have added 6 main color beads over each crystal.

Medium flower 2

Note: In this photo the beadwork is shown from the back. Weave the working thread so that it is coming out of a middle (third) bead on the first row of netting with 5 beads per point. Pick up 1 accent bead, a 4mm crystal and 1 accent bead. Then go through the middle bead of the next point. Repeat until there are 6 of the 4mm crystals. Then add 6 main color beads over each crystal following the previous step. Tie off the tail thread but leave the working thread attached.

Small flower 1

Start a new thread approximately 1½ yards (1.4m) long, single thickness with no knot. Repeat large flower steps 1–7. Then weave the working thread so that it is coming out of a middle (fourth) bead of the row of netting with 7 beads per point. Pick up 5 accent beads and go through the next middle bead of the next point. Repeat until you have added 6 sets of accent beads. End with the thread coming out of a middle (fourth) bead of the row with 7 beads per point.

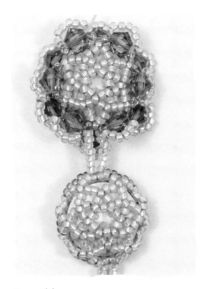

Small flower 2

Pick up 5 main color beads, a 4mm crystal and 1 main color bead, the drop bead, 1 main color bead, the 5mm crystal and 3 main color beads. Skip the last 3 main color beads and go back up the other beads, and come out of the fifth main color bead. Pick up 4 main color beads and go back through the middle bead of the point the thread originally exited from on the opposite side.

Assembly 1

Note: In this photo the beadwork is shown from the back. Weave the working thread on the small flower through the beadwork and come out of the middle (fourth) bead of the point with 7 beads directly across from the fringe. Pick up 7 main color beads and then go through the middle (third) bead of the first row of netting with 5 beads per point on the medium flower. Make sure the right sides of both flowers are on the same side. Pick up 7 main color beads and go back through the middle bead the thread originally exited from on the opposite side. Reinforce one more time. Tie off the tail and working thread on the small flower.

Assembly 2

Weave the working thread on the medium flower and come out of the middle (third) bead of the first row of netting with 5 beads per point that is directly across from the point where the small flower is connected. Pick up 12 main color beads and go through the 4mm crystal that is directly across from the bail on the large flower. Make sure the right sides of the flowers are on the same side. Pick up 12 main color beads and go back through the middle bead of the medium flower the thread originally exited from on the opposite side. Reinforce several times. Tie off any remaining threads on the flowers.

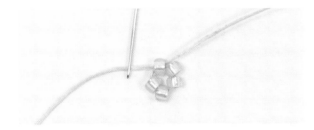

Rope strap 1

The rope strap is worked with odd-count tubular peyote (see page 18). There is no step up after each row; it just spirals around. Start a new thread about 2½ yards (2.3m) long, single thickness with no knot. Pick up 5 main color beads and go back through them again from the tail end. Also go through the first bead again to tighten the circle. Leave a 10" to 12" (25cm to 30cm) tail.

Rope strap 2

Pick up 1 main color bead, skip over the next bead and go through the next one. Repeat once more. Pick up 1 main color bead and go through the first bead added. The beads need to sit on top of each other. Keep picking up 1 main color bead, skip over the recessed bead and go through the next bead. The rope should start to spiral up. Be sure to pull each stitch snug.

Closure pattern 1

Once the rope is the desired length, the clasp bead will be added to one end. A good average length is approximately 12" (30cm). This rope tends to stretch a little when the pendant is put on it, so keep that in mind when deciding on the finished length. Weave the working thread through the last 5 beads at the end of the rope to pull them together. Pick up 5 main color beads, 1 accent bead, the 6mm bead and 3 more accent beads. Skip the last 3 accent beads and go back through the 6mm bead and the first accent bead. Pick up 5 more main color beads and go through a bead at the end of the rope across from where the thread originally exited. Reinforce. Tie off the working thread.

Closure pattern 2

On the other end of the rope, use the tail thread and go through the last 5 beads to pull them closer together. Pick up 5 main color beads, 1 accent bead and then enough main color beads to fit comfortably but snugly around the 6mm bead. Go back through the accent bead. Pick up 5 main color beads and go through a bead at the end of the rope across from where the thread originally exited. Reinforce. Tie off any remaining threads.

Ring

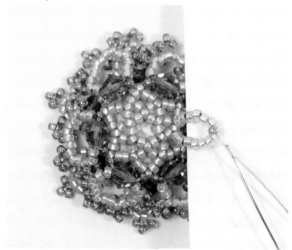

Ring pattern 1

Follow all steps through large flower step 14 of the pendant to make a large flower. Then weave the working thread so that it is coming out of the middle (second) bead of the first row of netting with 3 beads per point. Pick up 6 main color beads, 1 accent bead and 6 main color beads. Go back through the bead of the netting the thread originally exited from on the opposite side and also go through the first 6 main color beads and the accent bead. This will form a circle.

Ring pattern 2

Keep making circles following the previous step until the ring band is the desired length. A good average length is 7 circles (approximately a size-6 ring). Attach the last circle at the middle (second) bead of the first row of netting with 3 beads per point that is directly across from the point where you started the circles. Reinforce. Tie off any remaining threads.

Sequins in Symmetry Bracelet and Earrings

I had acquired quite a few vintage sequins that I wanted to use in a design. This delicate bracelet resulted. To jazz it up, you could use flat crystals in place of the sequins. Make it longer and you would have a pretty choker.

 **DIFFICULTY LEVEL**

Bracelet Materials

Size 12 beading needle

Size D Nymo beading thread or FireLine

(18) 6mm sequins, or more depending on desired length (Teal)

(2) 4mm round beads (Light Bronze)

6 grams size-8 Japanese seed beads (Matte Bronze AB)

9 grams size-15 Japanese seed beads for main color (Lined Light Aqua)

1 gram size-15 Japanese seed beads for accent color (Metallic Bronze)

Earring Materials

Size 12 beading needle

Size D Nymo beading thread or FireLine

Pair of earwires

(8) 6mm sequins (Teal)

(2) 15.5mm x 5mm dagger-style drop beads (Light Bronze)

3 grams size-8 Japanese seed beads (Matte Bronze AB)

4 grams size-15 Japanese seed beads for main color (Lined Light Aqua)

1 gram size-15 Japanese seed beads for accent color (Metallic Bronze)

Bracelet

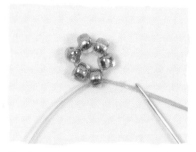

Circle pattern 1

Start with approximately 1 yard (.9m) of thread, single thickness with no knot. Pick up 6 main color beads and then go through all 6 beads again from the tail end. Leave a 8" to 10" (20cm to 25cm) tail. This will be used later to add a sequin to the top of the beadwork. Also go forward through the first bead again, to pull the little circle closer together. Do not pull the circle together too tightly; beads will be added in between the beads of the circle and they will need a little bit of room to fit in.

Circle pattern 2

Pick up 1 main color bead and go forward through the next main color bead of the original circle of 6 beads. Repeat 5 more times. After adding the last bead, also go through the first main color bead added in this row. This lines the thread up for the next row.

Circle pattern 3

Pick up 2 main color beads and go through the next main color bead from the last row of 6 main color beads. Repeat 5 more times. After adding the last set of 2 main color beads, also go through the first bead of the first set of 2 main color beads added in this row.

Circle pattern 4

Pick up 2 main color beads and then go down the next main color bead of the first set of 2 main color beads from the last row. Then go up the first main color bead of the next set of main color beads from the last row.

Circle pattern 5

Repeat the previous step 5 more times. After adding the last set of main color beads, also go through the first bead of the first set of main color beads from the last row, and through the first bead of the first set of main color beads added in this row.

Circle pattern 6

Pick up 2 main color beads and go down the next main color bead of the first set of main color beads from the last row. Pick up 1 size-8 bead and go up the first main color bead of the next set of main color beads from the last row. Repeat 5 more times. After adding the last size-8 bead, also go through the first bead of the first set of main color beads from the last row, and through the first bead of the first set of main color beads from the row just added.

Circle pattern 7

Pick up 3 main color beads and go down the next main color bead of the first set of main color beads from the last row. Also go forward through the size-8 bead. Pick up 3 main color beads and go back through the size-8 bead on the opposite side from where the thread originally exited. Also go up through the first bead of the next set of main color beads. This will make a picot on top of the size-8 bead.

Circle pattern 8

Repeat the previous step 5 more times.

Circle pattern 9

Weave the tail thread left earlier so that it is coming out of one of the main color beads from the original circle of 6 beads. Pick up 1 sequin and 1 accent bead. Skip the accent bead and go back down the sequin. Go through a main color bead of the original circle on the opposite side from where the thread originally exited from.

Circle pattern 10

Go back up the sequin and the accent bead, go down through the sequin, and go through the main color bead the thread originally started in on the opposite side from where it originally exited. The sequin should sit on top of the circle. Pull snug. Weave the tail in and tie it off. Leave the working thread attached.

Make another circle following circle pattern steps 1–10.

Assembly 1

Weave a working thread on one of the circles so that it is coming out of a middle bead of a main color picot over a size-8 bead. Pick up 1 size-8 bead and then go through a middle bead of a picot over a size-8 bead on the other circle. Then go back through the size-8 bead and also through the main color bead of the picot the thread originally exited from on the opposite side.

Assembly 2

Weave over to the middle bead of the picot over the next stack of beads without a size-8 bead. Circle stitch it to the middle bead of the corresponding picot on the other circle (see page 10).

Assembly 3

Weave over to the middle bead of the picot over the next size-8 bead and repeat assembly step 1.

Make 2 more circles following circle pattern steps 1–10, and connect them following assembly steps 1–3.

Assembly 4

The 2 sets of 2 circles are connected at the middle beads of the picots on the stacks of beads without a size-8 bead using circle stitches. Refer to the photo for the proper connection points of the circles.

Closure pattern 1

Keep making circles and connecting them together following all of the previous steps. Eighteen circles form a bracelet that is approximately 7½" (19cm) long. Add or subtract circles for a longer or shorter bracelet.

Once the bracelet is the desired length, the 4mm clasp beads need to be added. Refer to the photo for the proper middle beads of the picots of the stacks of main color beads to attach the 4mm beads to on the last circles. Weave a working thread so that it is coming out of the proper middle bead, then pick up 5 main color beads, 1 accent bead, a 4mm bead and 3 accent beads. Skip the 3 accent beads and go back through the 4mm bead and the next accent bead. Pick up 5 main color beads and then go back through the middle picot bead the thread originally exited from on the opposite side. Reinforce. Repeat on the other end circle.

Closure pattern 2

Refer to the photo for the proper placement of the clasp loops. Weave a working thread so that it is coming out of the middle picot bead of the proper stack, and pick up enough main color beads to fit comfortably but snugly around the 4mm bead. Then go back through the middle picot bead the thread originally exited from on the opposite side. Reinforce. Repeat on the other end circle. Tie off any remaining threads.

Earrings

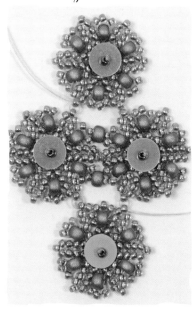

Earring pattern 1

Follow circle pattern steps 1–10 of the bracelet to make 4 circles. Then connect 2 of them following assembly steps 1–3 of the bracelet. Use circle stitches to connect the other 2 circles to the top and bottom of the 2 connected circles. Refer to the photo for the proper placement.

Earring pattern 2

Weave a working thread on one of the single circles so that it is coming out of the middle bead of the picot over the size-8 bead across from the connection to the set of 2 circles. Refer to the photo for proper placement. Pick up 5 main color beads, a drop bead and 5 main color beads. Go back through the middle bead that the thread originally exited from on the opposite side.

Earring pattern 3

Weave a working thread on the single circle opposite the circle where the drop bead was just added so that the working thread is coming out of the middle bead of the stack across from the connection to the set of 2 circles. Pick up 8 main color beads and an earwire and go back through the middle bead of the stack of main color beads across from the other connection point. Reinforce. Tie off any remaining threads.

Repeat all of these steps for the second earring.

Midnight Lace Necklace

This delicate necklace with a Victorian vibe is fairly easy to make and would suit many different outfits.

 DIFFICULTY LEVEL

Materials

Size 12 beading needle

Size D Nymo beading thread or FireLine

(14) 4mm bicone crystals (Gold)

(6) 5mm bicone crystals (Montana Blue)

6mm fire polish crystal (Blue Iris)

9 grams size-15 Japanese seed beads for main color (Blue Iris)

2 grams size-15 Japanese seed beads for accent color (Metallic Gold)

Large netted piece 1
Start with about 2 yards (1.8m) of thread, single thickness with no knot. Pick up 1 main color bead and turn it into a stop bead by going back through it from the tail end. Leave a 4" to 6" (10cm to 15cm) tail. Pick up 17 more main color beads for a total of 18 beads. Then go up through the fifth size-15 main color bead.

Large netted piece 2
Pick up 3 more main color beads and go up through the first main color bead.

Large netted piece 3
Pick up 3 main color beads and go down through the second bead (the middle bead) of the 3 main color beads picked up in the previous step. Pull snug.

Large netted piece 4
Pick up 15 main color beads and go back up the second bead just picked up. Pull snug.

Large netted piece 5
Pick up 3 main color beads and go through the middle bead of the previous group of 3 main color beads at the top of the netting. Pull snug.

Large netted piece 6
Repeat large netted piece steps 3-5 until there are 19 loops at the bottom of the netting. End with the working thread coming out of the top of the netting. This completes the large netted piece.

Now make 2 more pieces of netting with the main color beads following large netted piece steps 1-6, but with only 11 loops at the bottom of each piece. These are the smaller netted pieces. Tie off the tail threads but leave the working threads attached.

Assembly 1

Now the netted pieces need to be connected together. The working thread on a smaller netted piece should be coming out of the main color bead after the last 3 beads were added at the top of the netting. Pick up 1 accent bead, a 4mm crystal, 1 accent bead, a 5mm crystal, 1 accent bead, a 4mm crystal and 1 more accent bead. Then go through the main color stop bead and the next 11 main color beads at the other side of the small netted piece. This will bring the thread out of the middle (seventh) bead of the first loop on the netting.

Assembly 2

Go through the middle (seventh) main color bead on the first loop of the large netted piece. Then circle stitch it to the main color bead of the loop that the thread originally exited from (see page 10).

Assembly 3

Weave the working thread down to the second loop of the small netted piece and come out of the middle (seventh) main color bead. Pick up 1 accent bead, a 4mm crystal and 1 more accent bead. Then go through the middle (seventh) main color bead on the second loop on the large netted piece. Go back through the accent bead, the 4mm crystal and the next accent bead, and then go through the main color bead of the loop that the thread originally exited from on the opposite side.

Assembly 4

Weave the working thread down to the third loop of the small netted piece and come out of the middle (seventh) main color bead. Pick up 3 main color beads, 1 accent bead, a 4mm crystal, 1 accent bead, a 5mm crystal, 1 accent bead, a 4mm crystal, 1 accent bead and 3 main color beads. Then go through the middle (seventh) main color bead on the third loop on the large netted piece. Go back through the beads just picked up and also go through the main color bead of

the loop that the thread originally exited from on the opposite side.

Repeat assembly steps 1–4 with the other small netted piece on the other side of the large netted piece.

Assembly 5

The working thread on the large netted piece should be coming out of the main color bead after the last 3 main color beads were added at the top of the netting. Pick up 3 main color beads, 1 accent bead, a 4mm crystal, 1 accent bead, a 5mm crystal, 1 accent bead, a 4mm crystal, 1 accent bead and 3 main color beads. Then go through the stop bead at the end of the large netted piece. Reinforce.

Assembly 6

Weave the working thread over to the second main color bead that sticks out on the top edge of the large netted piece. Then pick up 5 main color beads, 1 accent bead, a 4mm crystal, 1 accent bead, a 5mm crystal, 1 accent bead, a 4mm crystal, 1 accent bead and 5 main color beads. Then go through the second bead on the other end of the large netted piece that sticks out, and also go back through the beads just picked up. Then go through the main color bead of the netted piece that the thread originally exited from on the opposite side. Reinforce.

Strap pattern

Now weave a working thread (or add a new thread) so that it is coming out of the middle (seventh) main color bead of the first loop on the small netted piece at the end of the necklace. Pick up 6 main color beads, 1 accent bead and 6 main color beads. Then go back through the main color bead of the loop that the thread originally exited from on the opposite side, and also go forward through the first 6 main color beads and the accent bead.

Keep repeating, adding circles until the strap is the desired length. The sample strap has 20 loops on each side and the necklace is approximately 15½" (39cm) long.

Repeat this step on the other small netted piece for the other strap.

Closure pattern 1

Now the clasp bead needs to be added to one end. The working thread should be coming out of the last accent bead on the last circle of one of the straps. Pick up 6 main color beads, 1 accent bead, the 6mm fire polish bead and 3 accent beads. Skip the 3 accent beads and go back through the 6mm bead and the next accent bead. Pick up 6 main color beads and go through the accent bead the thread originally exited from on the opposite side. Reinforce.

Closure pattern 2

The clasp loop needs to be added to the other strap. Weave the working thread so that it is coming out of the last accent bead on the last circle. Pick up enough main color beads to fit comfortably but snugly around the 6mm bead. Reinforce. Tie off any remaining threads.

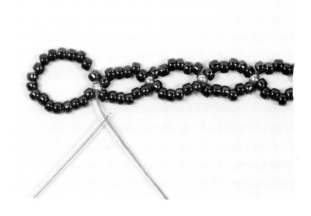

Drop Anklet

This fun and flirty anklet is a great accent for a summer outfit. If anklets aren't your thing, make it shorter and wear it as a bracelet. If you don't have any dagger-style drops, any top-drilled drops will work.

DIFFICULTY LEVEL

Materials

Size 12 beading needle

Size D Nymo beading thread or FireLine

(16) 15.5mm x 5mm dagger-style drop beads (Purple Iris)

(16) 3mm pearl beads (Gold Pearl)

6mm fire polish bead (Purple Iris)

4 grams size-11 Japanese seed beads for main color (Metallic Gold)

8 grams size-11 Japanese seed beads for accent color (Purple Iris Gold Luster)

Chain pattern 1
Start with approximately 2½ yards (2.3m) of thread, single thickness with no knot. Pick up 4 main color beads and go back through the first and second bead from the tail end. Leave a 10" to 12" (25cm to 30cm) tail. This will be used later to add the clasp bead. Pull snug.

Chain pattern 2
Pick up an accent color bead and go through the third and fourth bead of the original 4 main color beads. Pull snug.

Chain pattern 3
Pick up 4 main color beads and go back through the first 2 main color beads just picked up. Pull this snug and make sure that the beads are close to the previous group of beads.

Chain pattern 4
Pick up an accent color bead and go back through the 2 main color beads that the thread is coming out of on the same side, and also go through the next bead of the adjacent group. Pull snug.

Chain pattern 5
Pick up an accent color bead and go through the 2 main color beads that are next to the 3 you just went through. Pull snug.

Repeat chain pattern steps 3–5 until the chain is the desired length. A good average length is 8½" (22cm), before the clasp ends are added. **Note:** If you make the chain longer, you may need a few more drop and 3mm beads.

Closure pattern 1

Weave the working thread so that it is coming out of the last 2 main color beads at the end of the chain. Pick up 4 or 5 main color beads, the 6mm bead and 3 more main color beads. Skip the last 3 main color beads and go back through the 6mm bead and the next main color bead. Pick up 3 or 4 main color beads—the end beads are at a slight angle, so you may need to adjust the number of beads to get the 6mm clasp bead to lay straight—and go back through the end beads the thread originally exited from on the opposite side. Reinforce.

Closure pattern 2

Use the tail thread left in chain pattern step 1 to make a loop of main color beads on the other end of the chain that fits comfortably but snugly around the 6mm clasp bead. Reinforce. Weave in and tie off the tail thread.

Drop bead pattern 1

To add the drop beads, weave the working thread so that it is coming out of the first accent color bead on the edge of the chain. The drops will hang better if you use the accent color beads on the edge that allows them to sit straighter; on one side the accent color beads tend to twist a little. Use the other edge, where they lay in the same direction. Pick up 3 accent color beads and go through the next accent color bead on the edge of the chain.

Drop bead pattern 2

Pick up 3 accent color beads, a 3mm bead, 5 accent color beads, a drop bead and 5 accent color beads. Then go back up through the 3mm bead. Pick up 3 accent color beads, skip the next accent bead on the edge of the chain and go through the next one.

Keep repeating drop bead pattern steps 1–2 until you get to the end of the chain. Tie off any remaining threads.

Fringed Pendant and Bracelet

This necklace is all about the fringe. Straight fringe is mixed with embellished fringe for a full waterfall effect. If the fringe is a little too long for your tastes, you can always make it shorter. Even the bracelet has fringe of a sort in the strands that make up the band. Did I mention that I love fringe?

 DIFFICULTY LEVEL

Pendant Materials

Size 12 beading needle

Size D Nymo beading thread or FireLine

(96) 3mm glass pearls (Olivine)

(37) 3mm bicone crystals (Smoked Topaz)

(11) 4mm bicone crystals (Smoked Topaz)

(11) 7mm x 5mm drop beads (Smoked Topaz)

6mm round bead for clasp (Dark Bronze)

5 grams size-11 Japanese seed beads
for main color (Matte Metallic Olive Iris)

3 grams size-11 Japanese seed beads
for accent color (Metallic Dark Bronze)

8 grams size-15 Japanese seed beads
for main color (Matte Metallic Olive Iris)

9 grams size-15 Japanese seed beads
for accent color (Metallic Dark Bronze)

Bracelet Materials

Size 12 beading needle

Size D Nymo beading thread or FireLine

(58) 3mm glass pearls (Olivine)

(18) 3mm bicone crystals (Smoked Topaz)

(4) 4mm round beads for clasp beads (Dark Bronze)

2 grams size-11 Japanese seed beads
for main color (Matte Metallic Olive Iris)

2 grams size-11 Japanese seed beads
for accent color (Metallic Dark Bronze)

5 grams size-15 Japanese seed beads
for main color (Matte Metallic Olive Iris)

6 grams size-15 Japanese seed beads
for accent color (Metallic Dark Bronze)

Pendant

Rectangle pattern 1

Start with approximately 2 yards (1.8m) of thread, single thickness with no knot. Pick up 4 of the 3mm pearls. Then go back through all 4 pearls again from the tail end. Also go back through the first pearl again to pull them closer together. Leave a 4" to 6" (10cm to 15cm) tail. Pick up 3 more 3mm pearls and go back through the pearl that the thread originally exited from on the opposite side, and also go through the first 2 pearls of the 3 just added. Repeat once more.

Rectangle pattern 2

Pick up 3 more 3mm pearls and go back through the pearl that the thread originally exited from on the opposite side, and also go through the first pearl of the 3 pearls just added.

This is the first row of right-angle weave (see page 19). Try to think of each pearl as a side of a square with 4 pearls making up each square. There are 2 sides and a top and bottom to each square.

Rectangle pattern 3

Pick up 3 more 3mm pearls and go back through the pearl that the thread originally exited from on the opposite side. Also go through the 3 pearls just added, and then go through the top pearl of the next square.

Rectangle pattern 4

Pick up 2 more 3mm pearls and go through the side pearl of the previous square, and then go back through the pearl that the thread originally exited from on the opposite side. Also go through the first pearl of the 2 just added.

Rectangle pattern 5

Pick up 2 more 3mm pearls and go through the bottom pearl of the next square of the previous row, and then go back through the pearl that the thread originally exited from on the opposite side. Also go through the 2 pearls just added and the top pearl of the next square.

Rectangle pattern 6

Pick up 2 more 3mm pearls and go through the side pearl of the previous square, and then go back through the pearl that the thread originally exited from on the opposite side. Also go through the 2 pearls just added.

Rectangle pattern 7

Pick up 3 more 3mm pearls and go back through the pearl the thread originally exited from on the opposite side, and also go through the first pearl of the 2 just added.

Rectangle pattern 8

Pick up 2 more 3mm pearls and go through the bottom pearl of the next square of the previous row, and then go back through the pearl the thread originally exited from on the opposite side. Also go through the 2 pearls just added and the pearl of the next square.

Rectangle pattern 9

Pick up 2 more 3mm pearls and go through the side pearl of the previous square, and then go back through the pearl the thread originally exited from on the opposite side. Also go through the first pearl of the 2 just added.

Rectangle pattern 10

Pick up 2 more 3mm pearls and go through the bottom pearl of the next square of the previous row, and also go back through the pearl the thread originally exited from on the opposite side. Then go through the first pearl of the 2 just added.

Repeat rectangle pattern steps 3–10 to add 3 more rows. There should be a total of 6 rows.

Rectangle pattern 11

Now weave the working thread so that it is coming out of a pearl on the outside edge of the rectangle of beads. Pick up 1 size-11 main color bead and go through the next pearl on the edge of the rectangle. Repeat all the way around the rectangle.

Rectangle pattern 12

Weave the working thread so that it is coming out of the pearl below the end pearl on the top of the rectangle. It should be the pearl where the hole of the pearl is lined up with the next pearl. Pick up 1 size-11 main color bead and go through the next pearl. Repeat twice to complete the row, and then weave down to the next row and repeat.

Repeat until there are 15 size-11 main color beads added to the rectangle.

Rectangle pattern 13

Weave the working thread so that it is coming out of the second to last size-11 main color bead on the side of the rectangle toward the bottom. Pick up 1 size-15 main color bead, a 3mm crystal and 1 more size-15 main color bead. Then go through the second size-11 main color bead on the bottom of the rectangle.

Rectangle pattern 14

Go through the next 3mm pearl on the bottom edge of the rectangle. Then pick up 1 size-15 main color bead, a 3mm crystal and 1 size-15 main color bead, and go through the size-11 main color bead on top of the square. Pick up 1 size-15 main color bead, a 3mm crystal and 1 size-15 main color bead and go through the third size-11 main color bead on the side of the rectangle.

Rectangle pattern 15

Go through the next 3mm pearl on the side of the rectangle. Pick up 5 size-15 accent beads and go through the size-11 main color bead on top of the square. Repeat 2 more times and come out of the fourth size-11 main color bead on the bottom edge.

Rectangle pattern 16

Go through the next 3mm pearl on the bottom edge of the rectangle. Pick up 1 size-15 main color bead, a 3mm crystal and 1 size-15 main color bead and go through the size-11 main color bead on top of the square. Repeat 3 more times and come out of the fifth size-11 bead on the side of the rectangle.

Rectangle pattern 17

Go through the next 3mm pearl on the side of the rectangle. Pick up 1 size-15 main color bead, a 3mm crystal and 1 size-15 main color bead. Then go through the size-11 main color bead on top of the square. Repeat 3 more times and come out of the second size-11 main color bead on the side of the rectangle.

Rectangle pattern 18

Go through the next 3mm pearl on the side of the rectangle. Pick up 1 size-15 main color bead, a 3mm crystal and 1 size-15 main color bead. Then go through the size-11 main color bead on top of the square. Repeat 3 more times and come out of the size-11 main color bead on the top corner of the rectangle.

Rectangle pattern 19

Repeat the embellishments added in rectangle pattern steps 13–15, but in reverse order (work step 15, then 14, and end on 13).

Rectangle pattern 20

Weave the working thread so that it is coming out of the second size-11 main color bead on the side of the rectangle counting down from the top end of the rectangle. Pick up 3 size-11 accent beads and then go back through the size-11 main color bead the thread originally exited from on the opposite side. This will create a picot on the size-11 main color bead. Weave down to the next size-11 main color bead on the side and repeat. Repeat until there are 5 picots on the side. Weave over to the other side of the rectangle and repeat. There should be 5 picots on each side of the rectangle.

Fringe step 1

There are a total of 9 fringes on the pendant: 5 straight fringes which hang from the size-11 main color beads at the bottom of the rectangle, and 4 chain fringes which hang from the pearls at the bottom of the rectangle. The two types of fringe alternate back and forth.

Weave the working thread so that it is coming out of the first size-11 main color bead at the bottom end of the rectangle, working toward the rectangle. This is where the first straight fringe will hang.

The bead sequences for the first 3 straight fringes are listed on page 58. The third fringe is the longest. The fourth and fifth straight fringes are the same as the first and second straight fringes, just done in a mirror image (after the third fringe, do the sequence for the second fringe and then the first fringe to decrease back down).

After you pick up the fringe beads, skip the last 3 size-11 accent beads and go back up the remaining beads, then go through the size-11 main color bead of the rectangle on the opposite side from where the thread originally exited. This will make the straight fringe hang underneath the size-11 bead.

Now you need to begin a chain fringe. The working thread should be coming out of the first 3mm pearl on the

bottom edge of the rectangle after the size-11 main bead with the first straight fringe. Pick up 3 size-15 main color beads, 1 size-15 accent bead and 3 size-15 main color beads. Then go back through the 3mm pearl the thread originally exited from on the opposite side, and also go through the first 3 size-15 main color beads and the size-15 accent bead.

STRAIGHT FRINGE, BEAD SEQUENCE 1

3 size-15 main beads	12 size-11 main beads
size-11 accent bead	size-11 accent bead
3mm pearl	3mm pearl
size-11 accent bead	size-11 accent bead
3mm crystal	3mm crystal
size-11 accent bead	size-11 accent bead
3mm pearl	3mm pearl
size-11 accent bead	size-11 accent bead
6 size-11 main beads	12 size-11 main beads
size-11 accent bead	size-11 accent bead
3mm pearl	3mm crystal
size-11 accent bead	size-11 accent bead
4mm crystal	drop bead
size-11 accent bead	4 size-11 accent beads
3mm pearl	
size-11 accent bead	

STRAIGHT FRINGE, BEAD SEQUENCE 2

12 size-15 main beads	Repeat from * to
size-11 accent bead	* 1 more time
3mm pearl	size-11 accent bead
size-11 accent bead	3mm pearl
3mm crystal	size-11 accent bead
size-11 accent bead	4mm crystal
3mm pearl	size-11 accent bead
size-11 accent bead	3mm pearl
18 size-11 main beads	size-11 accent bead
*size-11 accent bead	12 size-11 main beads
3mm pearl	size-11 accent bead
size-11 accent bead	3mm crystal
4mm crystal	size-11 accent bead
size-11 accent bead	drop bead
3mm pearl	4 size-11 accent beads
size-11 accent bead	
18 size-11 main beads*	

STRAIGHT FRINGE, BEAD SEQUENCE 3

18 size-15 main beads	4mm crystal	3mm pearl
size-11 accent bead	size-11 accent bead	size-11 accent bead
3mm pearl	3mm pearl	20 size-11 main beads
size-11 accent bead	size-11 accent bead	size-11 accent bead
3mm crystal	20 size-11 main beads**	3mm crystal
size-11 accent bead	Repeat from ** to	size-11 accent bead
3mm pearl	** 2 more times	drop bead
size-11 accent bead	size-11 accent bead	4 size-11 accent beads
18 size-11 main beads	3mm pearl	
**size-11 accent bead	size-11 accent bead	
3mm pearl	3mm crystal	
size-11 accent bead	size-11 accent bead	

Fringe step 2

Continue the chain fringe. Pick up 3 size-15 main color beads, 1 size-15 accent bead and 3 size-15 main color beads. Then go back through the size-15 accent bead the thread originally exited from on the opposite side, and also go through the first 3 size-15 main color beads and the size-15 accent bead. Repeat for a total of 33 circles.

Then pick up 3 size-15 main color beads, 1 size-11 accent bead, a 3mm crystal, 1 size-11 accent bead, a drop bead and 4 size-11 accent beads. Skip the last 3 size-11 accent beads and go back up the next size-11 accent bead, the drop bead, the size-11 accent bead, the 3mm crystal and the next size-11 accent bead. Then pick up 3 size-15 main color beads and go back through the size-15 accent bead the thread originally exited from on the opposite side.

Fringe step 3

Pick up 3 size-15 accent beads and then go through the accent bead of the next circle. The size-15 accent beads just added will lay across the circle.

Fringe step 4

Keep repeating the previous step all the way up the circles. At the top, after adding the last 3 size-15 accent beads, go through the 3mm pearl and then pick up 3 size-15 accent beads and go through the size-15 accent bead of the next circle going back down the fringe. Now size-15 accent beads will be added to the back of the circles. Keep repeating all the way down the circles, adding 3 size-15 accent beads to the other side of each circle.

Note: The second chain fringe has 51 circles. The third chain fringe also has 51 circles, and the fourth goes back to 33 circles. The drop bead and the embellishing remain the same.

After working the first straight fringe and the first chain fringe, follow the appropriate patterns in fringe steps 1–4 to continue adding the remaining fringe, making sure to alternate between a straight fringe and a chain fringe.

Strap sections

Now you need to add the strap sections. They are done the same way as the chain fringe. Weave a working thread so that it is coming out of the end size-11 main color bead at the top of the rectangle. Pick up one of the drop beads, 1 size-11 accent bead, a 3mm crystal and 1 size-11 accent bead. Then make enough circles to fit comfortably around your neck. The sample necklace has 46 circles on each side and is approximately 8" (20cm) long on each side. (For the first circle, weave down through the drop bead and then back up to come out of the first size-15 accent bead of the first circle.) Then embellish the circles like the chain fringe following fringe steps 3–4.

Closure pattern 1

For the clasp, at the end of the first chain, pick up 3 size-11 main color beads, 1 size-11 accent bead, the 6mm bead and 3 size-11 accent beads. Skip the last 3 size-11 accent beads and then go back through the 6mm bead and the next size-11 accent bead. Pick up 3 size-11 main color beads and go back through the size-15 accent bead the thread originally exited from on the opposite side. Reinforce.

Closure pattern 2

On the other strap, after the last circle, add enough size-11 main color beads to fit comfortably but snugly around the 6mm bead. Reinforce. Tie off any remaining threads.

Bracelet

Bracelet pattern 1

Follow rectangle pattern steps 1–20 of the necklace to make the embellished rectangle. Then refer to fringe steps 1–2 to make the circles for the chain fringe on the first 3mm pearl on the rectangle. This chain makes up the band for the bracelet. The sample bracelet has 34 circles, and the finished length is approximately 6¾" (17cm) long. As the embellishments are added to the chain, it will shrink in length a little.

After the last circle is made, pick up 1 size-15 main color bead, 1 size-11 accent bead, 1 size-15 main color bead, a 4mm round bead and 3 size-15 main color beads. Skip the last 3 size-15 main color beads and go back through the other beads, and then go through the accent bead of the last circle that the working thread originally exited from on the opposite side.

Bracelet pattern 2

Follow fringe steps 3–4 to add the accent beads to the chain. Then weave over to the next 3mm pearl and repeat the steps to create another fringe. Repeat 2 more times. There are a total of 4 chains for the band of the bracelet.

Then add a new thread at the other end of the rectangle, approximately 1 yard (.9m) long, single thickness with no knot. It should be coming out of the first 3mm pearl on the end of the rectangle going toward the rectangle. Pick up enough size-15 accent beads to fit comfortably but snugly around the 4mm round bead at the end of the chain. Then go back through the 4mm bead on the opposite side from where the thread originally exited. Reinforce. Then weave over to the next 3mm pearl and repeat. Repeat 2 more times.

There should be 4 circles at the end of the rectangle for the 4mm beads to fit into for the clasps. Tie off any remaining threads. **Note:** To adjust the length of the bracelet, simply add or subtract the number of circles on the chains.

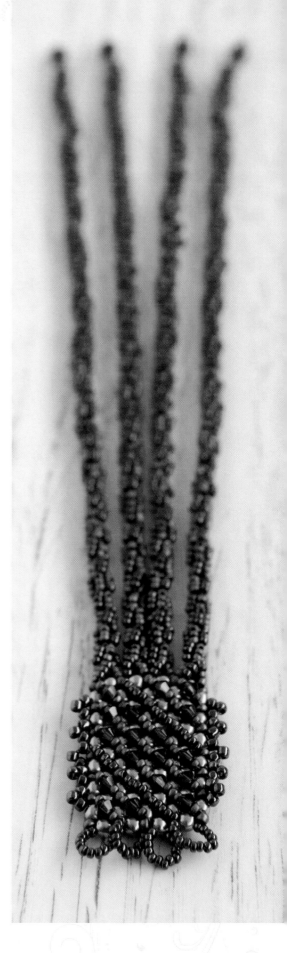

Crystal Flower Necklace

This asymmetrical necklace fastens in the front, so it is easy to put on. The center of the flower is a crystal rivoli, one of my favorite elements to work with. It adds a nice touch of bling to the design. The strap is a unique picot rope that is a little time-consuming to make, but beautiful.

 DIFFICULTY LEVEL

Materials

Size 12 beading needle

Size D Nymo beading thread or Fireline

(29) 4mm bicone crystals (Fuchsia)

(3) 9mm x 6mm smooth drop beads (Light Bronze)

(2) 6mm rondelles (Light Bronze)

18mm rivoli crystal (Volcano)

19 grams size-15 Japanese seed beads for main color (Metallic Bronze Iris)

Rope pattern 1
Start with approximately 2½ yards (2.3m) of thread, single thickness with no knot. Pick up 1 main color bead and turn it into a stop bead by going back through it from the tail end. Leave a 10" to 12" (25cm to 30cm) tail. Pick up 6 main color beads, then go back through the third bead of the 6 just picked up in a circular thread path. This will make a picot. Pull it snug against the other beads.

Rope pattern 2
Pick up 6 main color beads and go through the third bead of the 6 just picked up to make another picot. Pull it snug against the other picot. Repeat one more time. Then pick up 2 main color beads.

Rope pattern 3
Now turn the beads into a circle by going through the first bead (the stop bead).

Rope pattern 4
Now the beadwork will start to form a tube or rope. Pick up 5 main color beads and go through the second bead just picked up to make a picot. Pick up 1 main color bead. Pull the beads snug against the other beads. Then go through the tip bead of the next picot from the first row. Work in a circular thread path. Pull snug.

Rope pattern 5
Repeat rope pattern step 4 two more times.

Rope pattern 6
Keep adding picots following rope pattern steps 4–5. The rope will spiral up as the picots are added. Keep repeating until the rope is the desired length. A good average length is 17½" (44cm).

Flower pattern 1

Start a new thread, approximately 2 yards (1.8m) long, single thickness with no knot. Pick up 30 main color beads and go back through them from the tail end to create a circle. Leave a 4" to 6" (10cm to 15cm) tail. Go through a few more beads to pull the circle closer together. Pick up 7 main color beads. Count over 5 beads on the original circle and go through the fifth bead. Repeat 5 more times. There should now be 6 points around the circle. After the last point is added, also go through the first 4 beads of the first point that was added in this row. This lines the working thread up for the next row.

Flower pattern 2

Pick up 13 main color beads and go through the middle (fourth) bead of the next point from the last row. Repeat 5 more times. After the last point is added, also go through the first 7 beads of the first point added in this row.

Flower pattern 3

Pick up 7 main color beads and go through the middle (seventh) bead of the next point from the last row. Repeat 5 more times. This row will make the beadwork curl up. Insert the 18mm rivoli crystal into the beadwork and pull it snug. Reinforce this row one more time.

Flower pattern 4

Weave the working thread so that it is coming out of a third bead away from the last row of beads. Crystals are now going to be added between the beads of the previous row. Note that there are some smaller and some larger spaces as you look at the beadwork. For the larger spaces, pick up 1 main color bead, a 4mm crystal and 1 main color bead. Then go through the third bead of the next group of beads. For the smaller spaces, pick up a 4mm crystal and go through the third bead of the next group of beads. Alternate between adding the main beads with a crystal and just a crystal. There will be 12 crystals added in this row.

Flower pattern 5

Weave the working thread so that it is coming out of one of the crystals. Pick up 8 main color beads and then go through the fifth bead of the 8 just added to make a picot. Pull snug. Pick up 4 main color beads and go back through the crystal on the opposite side from where the thread originally exited. Weave over to the next crystal. Repeat 11 more times. There should be a picot over each crystal. Tie off the tail thread but leave the working thread attached.

Assembly 1

The tail thread on the rope should be coming out of the original circle of main color beads. Flatten the end of the rope and sew the end beads of the rope to the first circle of netting on the back of the flower using a circle stitch. Reinforce.

Closure pattern 1

The 6mm rondelle beads are sewn to the rope on the other end. Weave the working thread so that it is coming out of a bead near the end of the rope. Pick up 1 main color bead, a 6mm rondelle and 1 main color bead. Skip the main color bead and go back down the rondelle and the first main color bead. Then go back through the bead of the rope your thread originally exited from on the opposite side. Reinforce. Repeat with the other clasp bead about ½" (13mm) away from the first clasp bead.

Closure pattern 2

Weave the working thread from the flower so that it is coming out of a bead where the rope was attached. Pick up enough main color beads to fit comfortably but snugly around the 6mm rondelle bead. Go back through the bead of the flower on the opposite side from where the thread originally exited. Reinforce. Make 1 more loop across from the first loop. This loop is also attached to the beads of the flower. (Refer to the photo for proper placement.) Weave in and tie off the working thread.

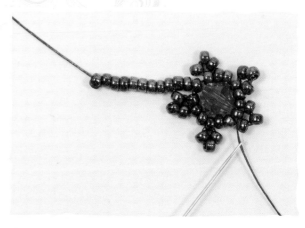

Flower string 1

Start a new thread, approximately 2 yards (1.8m) long, single thickness with no knot. Pick up 1 main color bead and turn it into a stop bead by going back through it from the tail end. Leave a 4" to 6" (10cm to 15cm) tail. Pick up 15 more main color beads and go through the twelfth bead of the 15 beads just picked up. This will make a picot. Pull it snug against the other beads. Pick up 6 main color beads and go through the third bead of the 6 beads just picked up to make another picot. Repeat for a total of 5 picots.

Flower string 2

Go back through the first main color bead before the first picot in a circular thread path. This will make a circle out of the picots. Pick up a 4mm crystal and go through the bottom bead of the third picot.

Flower string 3

Pick up 16 main color beads and repeat flower string steps 1–2 to make 5 more picots with a crystal in the center. Repeat for a total of 5 picot flowers.

Flower string 4

Weave the working thread so that it is coming out of one of the main color beads between the last 2 flowers. Pick up 9 main color beads, then skip the last bead just picked up and go back through the next bead. Pick up 6 beads and go through the first main color bead of the 9 beads. This creates a leaf.

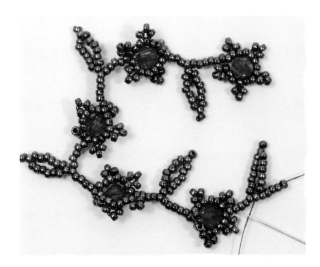

Flower string 5

Weave the working thread over to the next group of main color beads between the flowers and repeat flower string step 4. Keep repeating, adding a leaf between each flower and 1 after the last flower.

Assembly 2

Then attach one end of the string of flowers to the rope by tacking it to the end of the rope where the large crystal flower is attached. Loosely wrap the flowers around the rope and tack it down to a main color bead at the end. You may also want to tack it down in several places in the middle to help hold it in place.

Flower fringe

Weave a working thread on the other end of the rope so that it is coming out of one of the tip beads of the picots. Then make a fringe following flower string steps 1–5; however, at the end, before you go back up and add the leaves, add a drop bead with 3 main color beads as the turnaround beads.

There are 3 fringes: make 1 with 5 flowers, 1 with 4 flowers and 1 with 3 flowers. Each fringe hangs from a tip of a picot bead. Tie off any remaining threads.

Mobile Necklace and Earrings

Sometimes I have a really hard time coming up with names for my pieces, but this necklace reminded me of a mobile so that is what I called it. The necklace has five dangles, but for a greater wow factor you could easily add more.

 DIFFICULTY LEVEL

Necklace Materials

Size 12 beading needle

Size D Nymo beading thread or FireLine

Approximately 3" (8cm) of 2.2mm sterling silver flat cable chain

(5) 4mm bicone crystals (Tanzanite)

(5) 9mm x 6mm drop beads (Tanzanite)

8mm fire polish bead for clasp (Smoke/Crystal)

6 grams size-15 Japanese seed beads for main color (Steel Blue Gold Luster Iris)

4 grams size-11 Japanese seed beads for accent color (Purple Gold Luster Iris)

4 grams size-11 Japanese cylinder beads for diamonds (Grey Transparent Iris)

Earring Materials

Size 12 beading needle

Size D Nymo beading thread or FireLine

Approximately 3" (8cm) of 2.2mm sterling silver flat cable chain

Pair of sterling earwires

(6) 4mm bicone crystals (Tanzanite)

(6) 9mm x 6mm drop beads (Tanzanite)

1 gram size-15 Japanese seed beads for main color (Steel Blue Gold Luster Iris)

1 gram size-11 Japanese seed beads for accent color (Purple Gold Luster Iris)

3 grams size-11 Japanese cylinder beads for diamonds (Grey Transparent Iris)

Necklace

Chain pattern 1
Start with approximately 2½ yards (2.3m) of thread, single thickness with no knot. Pick up 1 main color bead and go back through it from the tail end to turn it into a stop bead. Leave a 12" (30cm) tail. Then pick up 7 main color beads and 1 accent bead. Also go back through the first 4 main color beads, including the stop bead.

Chain pattern 2
Pick up 1 main color bead, 1 accent bead and 4 more main color beads. Then skip over the next 2 main color beads of the original circle and go through the next main color bead of the original circle.

Chain pattern 3
Pick up 1 main color bead, 1 accent bead and 4 more main color beads. Then skip over the first 2 main color beads from the group of 4 in the last row and go through the third main color bead from the last row. Repeat until the chain is the desired length. The sample necklace is approximately 15" (38cm) long.

Closure pattern 1
Once the chain is the desired length, the clasp bead needs to be added to one end. The working thread should be coming out of the last stitch. Pick up 5 main color beads, 1 accent bead, the 8mm fire polish bead and 3 accent beads. Then skip the 3 accent beads and go back through the 8mm bead and the next accent bead. Pick up 5 more main color beads and go through the 3 main color beads that are in front of the main color bead that the thread originally exited from. Reinforce.

Closure pattern 2
On the other end of the chain, use the tail thread to add the clasp loop. The thread should be coming out of the main color bead it started in. Pick up enough main color beads to fit comfortably but snugly around the 8mm bead. Then go through the 3 main color beads that are in front of the main color bead that the thread originally started in. Reinforce. Set the chain aside for now.

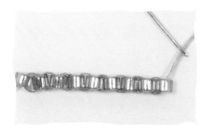  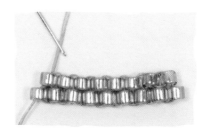

Diamond pattern 1

Start with approximately 1½ yards (1.4m) of thread, single thickness with no knot. Pick up 2 cylinder diamond beads and go back through them from the tail end. They should sit side by side. Leave a 4" to 6" (10cm to 15cm) tail. Pick up 1 cylinder diamond bead and go back through the last bead added on the opposite side from where the thread originally exited, and also go through the bead just picked up. This will make the new bead sit next to the other beads. Keep adding beads this way for a total of 9 cylinder diamond beads.

Diamond pattern 2

Pick up 2 cylinder diamond beads and go under the second thread from the back to the front and up the second bead. Go down the first cylinder diamond bead added and come back up the second cylinder diamond bead. This will make the beads sit closer together.

Diamond pattern 3

Pick up 1 cylinder diamond bead and go under the next thread from the back to the front and back up the bead just added. Keep adding beads this way until there are 8 beads in this row.

Diamond pattern 4

Keep working rows following diamond pattern steps 2–3 until you get to a row of 2 beads. (Each row will decrease by one bead.) Then pick up 1 cylinder diamond bead, catch the thread between the last row of 2 beads, and go back up the bead just added.

Diamond pattern 5

Weave the working thread down the side of the triangle and come out of an end bead on the row with 9 beads. Continue making rows on this side of the triangle following diamond pattern steps 2–4. You now have a large diamond shape with 1 bead on each end. Leave the tail and working threads attached.

Make 1 more diamond this size. There are 2 on the necklace.

Small diamond

Follow diamond pattern steps 1–5 to make 4 small diamonds. However, work the first step with a total of 7 beads. Each diamond should end with 1 bead per row.

Assembly 1

Now the drop beads and chain need to be added to the diamonds. Weave the working thread on a large diamond so that it is coming out of a single bead at one end. Pick up a 4mm crystal, 1 cylinder diamond bead, a drop bead and 3 accent beads. Skip the last 3 accent beads and go back up the other beads. Weave the working thread in and tie it off.

Assembly 2

Weave the tail thread on the same diamond so that it is coming out of the single cylinder diamond bead at the other end of the diamond. Cut a piece of chain so that it has 6 links. Circle stitch the end link on the chain to the single cylinder diamond bead the thread originally exited from. Tie off the tail thread.

Assembly 3

Repeat assembly steps 1–2 on 2 of the small diamonds. However, cut the chain so there are 10 links for the 2 small diamonds.

On the other 2 small diamonds, add the fringe sequence, but do not add a chain at the top.

Assembly 4

Weave the working thread on the large diamond with no chain or drops so that it is coming out of a single cylinder diamond bead at one end. Then go through the end link of the chain on the large diamond that has the chain attached. Then go back through the cylinder diamond bead the thread originally exited, and then weave through the beads of the diamond and bring the working thread out of the single cylinder diamond bead on the other end. Tie off the tail thread.

Assembly 5

Fold the strap in half to find the accent bead that is closest to the center. The working thread on the connected large diamonds should be coming out of the single cylinder diamond bead at the end. Pick up 1 accent bead and 3 main color beads. Then go through the center accent bead on the strap. Pick up 3 main color beads and go back through the accent bead and the single cylinder diamond bead of the diamond. Reinforce one more time.

Assembly 6
Weave the working thread from the large diamond through the strap and come out of the third accent bead of the strap, counting over from the connection of the large diamonds. Then circle stitch it to the end link of the chain on one of the small diamonds. Reinforce one more time.

Assembly 7
Weave the working thread on one of the small diamonds with no chain so that it is coming out of the single cylinder diamond bead at the end. Pick up 1 accent bead and 3 main color beads. Then go through the third accent bead on the strap, counting over from the connection of the small diamond with the chain connected in assembly step 6. Pick up 3 main color beads, and go back through the accent bead just picked up and the cylinder accent bead of the diamond. Reinforce one more time. Tie off the working thread.

Repeat assembly steps 6–7 with the other small diamonds for the other half of the necklace. Remember, it should be a mirror image. Tie off any remaining threads.

Earrings

Earring pattern 1
Follow diamond pattern steps 1–4 of the necklace to make a triangle. The first row should have a total of 7 cylinder diamond beads. End the triangle with a row of 2 beads.

Make one more triangle this size (you need two for the earrings). Tie off the tail threads. Set the triangles aside for now.

Earring pattern 2
Make 6 diamonds following diamond pattern steps 1–5 of the necklace—however, the first row should have a total of 5 beads. You will only need about 1 yard (.9m) of thread. One end of each diamond should be a row with a single bead, and the other end should be a row of 2 beads. Weave in and tie off the tail threads.

Earring pattern 3

The working thread on each diamond should be coming out of an end bead on the end with 2 beads per row. Pick up 3 cylinder diamond beads, a 4mm crystal, 1 accent bead, a drop bead and 3 more accent beads. Skip the last 3 accent beads and go back up the other beads. Then go through the other end bead on the 2-bead row. This will make the drop beads hang between the two beads of the last row. Then weave through the beads and come out of the single bead on the other end.

Cut a piece of chain with 3 links. Circle stitch an end link of the chain to the single bead at the end of the diamond. Weave in the working thread and tie it off.

Add the drop beads and 3 pieces of chain with 3 links to 3 more diamonds. There are 4 of these diamonds on the earrings. Then make 2 diamond shapes with the drop beads, but cut the chain so it has 6 links instead of 3, and add those to the last 2 diamond shapes.

Earring pattern 4

The working thread on the triangles should be coming out of one of the 2 beads on the 2-bead row. Pick up 6 main color beads and go through the loop of an earwire. Then go through the other end bead of the 2-bead row. Reinforce. Repeat on the other triangle.

Earring pattern 5

Weave the working thread on a triangle so that it is coming out of the end bead on the 7-bead row. Go through the last link on a diamond with a 3-link chain attached. Then go back up the end bead, go down the second bead of the row, go up the third bead, and then come out of the fourth bead of the row. Go through the end loop on a diamond with a 6-link chain attached. Then go back up the fourth bead, go down the fifth bead, up the sixth bead, and come down out of the seventh bead (the other end bead). Then pick up a diamond with a 3-link chain attached. Go back up the seventh bead. Repeat with the 3 remaining diamonds on the other triangle for the other earring. Tie off any remaining threads.

Rivoli Flowers Bracelet

I don't think there can ever be too many ways to incorporate crystal rivolis into beading designs. They come in such wonderful colors and can be adapted to so many different techniques. This bracelet incorporates flat round peyote and netting to make the bezels for the rivolis.

DIFFICULTY LEVEL

Materials

Size 12 beading needle

Size D Nymo beading thread or FireLine

(12) 4mm or 5mm faceted rondelles (Blue Iris)

(7) 16mm crystal rivolis (Heliotrope)

6mm round bead for clasp (Purple Iris)

9 grams size-15 Japanese seed beads for main color (Metallic Purple)

6 grams size-15 Japanese seed beads for accent color 1 (Orchid AB)

6 grams size-15 Japanese seed beads for accent color 2 (Silver-Lined Teal AB)

Flower pattern 1
Start with approximately 2½ yards (2.3m) of thread, single thickness with no knot. Pick up 3 main color beads and then go back through them again from the tail end. Also go forward through the first bead again. Leave a 4" to 6" (10cm to 15cm) tail.

Flower pattern 2
Pick up 2 main color beads and go through the next main color bead from the previous row. Repeat two more times. There should be a total of 6 main color beads in this row. After the last beads are added, also go forward through the first bead added in this row. This technique is flat round peyote (see page 17).

Flower pattern 3
Pick up 1 accent #1 bead and go through the next main color bead from the previous row. Repeat until there are 6 accent #1 beads in this row. After the last bead is added, also go forward through the first bead added in this row.

Flower pattern 4
Pick up 2 main color beads and go through the next accent #1 bead from the previous row. Repeat until there are 12 main color beads in this row. After the last beads are added, also go forward through the first bead added in this row.

Flower pattern 5
Pick up 1 accent #1 bead and go through the next main color bead from the previous row. Repeat until there are 12 accent #1 beads in this row. After the last bead is added, also go forward through the first bead added in this row.

Flower pattern 6
Pick up 1 main color bead and go through the next accent #1 bead from the previous row. Repeat until there are 12 main color beads in this row. After the last bead is added, also go forward through the first bead added in this row.

Flower pattern 7
Pick up 2 accent #1 beads and go through the next main color bead from the previous row. Repeat until there are 24 accent #1 beads in this row. After the last beads are added, also go forward through the first 2 accent #1 beads added in this row.

Flower pattern 8
Pick up 1 main color bead and go through the next 2 accent #1 beads from the last row. Repeat until there are 12 main color beads in this row. After the last bead is added, also go forward through the first main color bead added in this row.

Flower pattern 9
Pick up 3 main color beads and go through the next main color bead from the last row. Repeat until there are 12 points of 3 main color beads in this row. After the last beads are added, also go forward through the first 2 main color beads of this row.

Flower pattern 10
Pick up 5 main color beads and go through the middle (second) bead of the next point of main color beads from the previous row. Repeat until there are 12 points with 5 main color beads in this row. After the last beads are added, also go forward through the first 3 main color beads of this row.

Flower pattern 11
Pick up 7 main color beads, skip over the next point from the previous row, and then go through the middle (third) bead of the next point from the previous row. Repeat 5 more times. There should be 6 sets of 7 beads in this row. After the last beads are added, also go forward through the first 4 main color beads of this row. Insert a 16mm rivoli into the beadwork and pull snug.

Flower pattern 12
Pick up 5 main color beads and go through the middle (fourth) bead of the next set of 7 beads from the previous row. Repeat 5 more times. Pull snug.

Flower pattern 13

The working thread should be coming out of the fourth bead of a set of 7 beads that were added in flower pattern step 11. Pick up 3 accent #1 beads and go back through the bead the thread originally exited from on the opposite side. This will make a picot. Weave over to the third bead of the next set of 5 beads added in flower pattern step 12. Pick up 3 accent #1 beads and go back through the bead the thread originally exited from on the opposite side. Repeat this step until there are 12 picots.

Flower pattern 14

Weave the working thread so that it is coming out of the middle (third) bead of a point with 5 beads from flower pattern step 10. Pick up 3 accent #2 beads and go through the middle bead of the next point with 5 beads (it will be a point that was skipped earlier when flower pattern step 11 was done). Then pick up 3 accent #2 beads and go through the middle bead of the next point of 5 beads (this one will be connected to the row of 7 beads). Repeat until there are 12 sets of accent #2 beads around the rivoli.

Flower pattern 15

The working thread should now be coming out of a middle (third) bead of a set of 5 beads from flower pattern step 10. Pick up 3 main color beads and go back through the bead the thread originally exited from on the opposite side. This will make a picot. Weave over to the middle (second) of the next set of 3 accent #2 beads added in the previous row. Pick up 3 accent #2 beads and then go back through the bead the thread originally exited from on the opposite side. Repeat until there are 24 picots of alternating colors.

Flower pattern 16

Weave the working thread so that it is coming out of the middle bead of a main color picot. Pick up 3 main color beads and go back through the bead the thread originally exited from on the opposite side. Also go down through the third bead of the previous main color picot, and then go up through the first and second bead of the next accent #2 picot. Pick up 3 accent #2 beads and then go through the bead the thread originally exited from on the opposite side.

Keep repeating, adding picots on top of the existing picots until all 24 picots have another picot added to the top. This completes one flower.

Repeat flower pattern steps 1–16 to make 6 more flowers (there are 7 on the bracelet). Tie off the tail threads but leave the working threads attached.

Assembly 1

Weave a working thread on one of the flowers so that it is coming out of the middle bead of a point with 3 beads that was created in flower pattern step 9. Pick up 1 main color bead, 1 accent #2 bead, a 5mm rondelle, 1 accent #2 bead and 1 main color bead. Then go through the middle bead of a 3-bead point on another flower. Then pick up 1 main color bead and go through the next accent #2 bead, the rondelle and the next accent #2 bead. Then pick up 1 main color bead and go through the point bead the thread originally exited from on the opposite side. Reinforce.

Assembly 2

Weave over, skipping the next 3-bead point, and come out of the next one. Then repeat assembly step 1. There are two connections between each flower, with a 3-bead point in between them. Reinforce. Repeat with the other flowers until they are all connected.

Seven flowers make a bracelet that is approximately 7" (18cm) long. For a longer bracelet, add another flower or a few more seed beads on the connections.

Closure pattern 1

Weave the working thread so that it is coming out of the fifth 3-bead point on the last flower on one end counting away from a connection. Pick up 3 main color beads, 1 accent #2 bead, the 6mm bead and 3 accent #2 beads. Skip the 3 accent #2 beads and go back through the 6mm bead and the next accent #2 bead. Then pick up 3 main color beads and go through the point bead the thread originally exited from on the opposite side. Reinforce.

Closure pattern 2

Weave the working thread on the flower on the other end so that it is coming out of the fifth 3-bead point counting away from a connection. Pick up enough main color beads to fit comfortably but snugly around the 6mm bead. Reinforce. Tie off any remaining threads.

Ruffled Rings Necklace

This piece is a fairly simple design, but by using gold metallic and lined beads it becomes quite elegant. I love long chain necklaces, and this is my beaded version of one. It is also easy to make longer or shorter by adjusting the number of circles.

 DIFFICULTY LEVEL

Materials

Size 12 beading needle

Size D Nymo beading thread or FireLine

(320) 3mm pearls (Gold)

14 grams size-11 Japanese seed beads for main color (Metallic Gold)

9 grams size-11 Japanese seed beads for accent color (Gold/Lined)

10 grams size-15 Japanese seed beads for main color (Metallic Gold)

24 grams size-15 Japanese seed beads for accent color (Gold/Lined)

Large ring pattern 1

Start with approximately 2 yards (1.8m) of thread, single thickness with no knot. Pick up 28 size-15 main color beads. Then go back through all of them again from the tail end. Also go forward through the first bead again to pull the circle closer together. Leave a 4" to 6" (10cm to 15cm) tail. Then pick up 1 size-15 main color bead, skip over a bead and go through the next one (flat round peyote stitch; see page 17). Repeat all the way around the circle for a total of 14 beads. After adding the last bead, also go through the first bead added in this row.

Large ring pattern 2

Pick up 1 size-11 accent bead and go through the next size-15 main color bead from the previous row. Repeat until there are 14 size-11 accent beads in this row. After adding the last bead, also go through the first bead added in this row.

Large ring pattern 3

Pick up 2 size-15 accent beads, 1 size-11 main color bead and 2 more size-15 accent beads and go through the next size-11 accent bead from the previous row. Repeat until there are 14 points in this row.

Large ring pattern 4

The working thread should be coming out of a size-11 accent bead from large ring pattern step 2. Pick up 5 size-15 accent beads and go through the next size-11 accent bead from large ring pattern step 2. Repeat until there are 14 points with the 5 size-15 accent beads in this row.

Large ring pattern 5

The next row of points is added to the other side of the circle, so poke the needle and thread through the beadwork and come out on the other side. This means you will be going in the opposite direction for this row. The working thread should be coming out of a size-11 accent bead from large ring pattern step 2. Pick up 5 size-15 accent beads and go through the next size-11 accent bead from large ring pattern step 2.

Repeat until there are 14 points with the size-15 accent beads in the row on this side of the circle. There are 3 rows (large ring pattern steps 3–5) of points around the peyote circle, and they are all added on the size-11 accent beads added in large ring pattern step 2. The row of points made in large ring pattern step 3 should end up in the middle of the 3 rows. Tie off the tail and working thread. This completes a large circle.

Make 19 more large circles. There are 20 of these large circles on the necklace.

Small ring pattern 1

Repeat large ring pattern step 1 but instead of 28 beads, pick up 24 size-15 main color beads. The next row will have 12 beads instead of 14.

Small ring pattern 2

Pick up 1 size-11 accent bead and go through the next size-15 main color bead from the previous row. Repeat until there are 12 size-11 accent beads in this row. After adding the last bead, also go through the first bead added in this row.

Small ring pattern 3

Pick up 1 size-15 accent bead, 1 size-11 main color bead and 1 more size-15 accent bead and go through the next size-11 accent bead from the previous row. Repeat until there are 12 points in this row.

Small ring pattern 4

The working thread should be coming out of a size-11 accent bead from small ring pattern step 2. Pick up 3 size-15 accent beads and go through the next size-11 bead from small ring pattern step 2. Keep repeating until there are 12 points with the 3 size-11 accent beads in this row.

Small ring pattern 5

The next row of points is added to the other side of the circle, so poke the needle and thread through the beadwork and come out on the other side. This means you will be going in the opposite direction for this row. The working thread should be coming out of a size-11 accent bead from small ring pattern step 2. Pick up 3 size-15 accent beads and go through the next size-11 accent bead from small ring pattern step 2.

Repeat until there are 12 points with the size-15 accent beads in the row on this side of the circle. This completes a small circle. Tie off the tail and working thread.

Make 19 more small circles. There are 20 of these small circles on the necklace.

Assembly 1

Now the circles need to be connected. Start a new thread approximately 1 yard (.9m) long, single thickness with no knot. Pick up 1 size-11 main color bead and a 3mm pearl. Repeat until you have 8 of each bead.

Assembly 2

Go through the center opening of a small circle and a large circle. Then go back through all the beads picked up in assembly step 1 from the tail end several times. Tie off the tail and working thread.

Repeat assembly steps 1–2 until you have all the circles connected. Be sure to alternate the large and small circles. Tie off any remaining threads.

Flower Garland Necklace and Bracelet

I don't usually put a lot of larger glass beads between my beadweaving components, but I like the way the 8mm round beads offset the dimensional flowers in this design. If you want to make the necklace longer, add more of the 8mm beads on each side.

 **DIFFICULTY LEVEL**

Necklace Materials

Size 12 beading needle

Size D Nymo beading thread or FireLine

(27) 5mm bicone crystals (Amethyst)

(20) 8mm round beads (Purple Luster)

20 grams size-11 Japanese seed beads for main color (Gold Luster Olive)

14 grams size-11 Japanese seed beads for accent color (Metallic Dark Purple)

10 grams size-15 Japanese seed beads for accent color (Metallic Dark Purple)

Bracelet Materials

Size 12 beading needle

Size D Nymo beading thread or FireLine

(12) 5mm bicone crystals (Amethyst)

(9) 8mm round beads (Purple Luster)

8 grams size-11 Japanese seed beads for main color (Gold Luster Olive)

9 grams size-11 Japanese seed beads for accent color (Metallic Dark Purple)

4 grams size-15 Japanese seed beads for accent color (Metallic Dark Purple)

Necklace

Flower pattern 1

Start with approximately 2 yards (1.8m) of thread, single thickness with no knot. Pick up 7 main color beads and then go back through them from the tail end to make a circle. Also go forward through 1 more bead to close the gap of thread at the end of the circle. Do not pull the circle together tightly, as beads are going to be added in between. Leave a 4" to 6" (10cm to 15cm) tail.

Pick up 1 main color bead and go through the next main color bead of the circle. Repeat until you have added 7 main color beads, one between each main color bead of the original circle. After adding the seventh main color bead, also go through the first main color bead added in this row.

Flower pattern 2

Pick up 2 main color beads and go through the next main color bead of the previous row. Repeat until there are 2 beads (a total of 14 beads in this row) between each bead of the last row. After adding the last 2 main color beads, also go through the first bead of the first 2 beads added in this row.

Flower pattern 3

The next row starts flat herringbone stitch (see page 15). Pick up 2 main color beads and then go down the next main color bead, then come up the next one. Repeat until there are 7 sets of 2 main color beads.

Flower pattern 4

Pick up 2 main color beads and go down the next main color bead from the last row. Then pick up 1 size-11 accent bead and go up through the next main color bead. The accent bead is an increase in the herringbone. Repeat until there are 7 sets of 2 main color beads with 7 size-11 accent beads in between each set.

Flower pattern 5

Pick up 2 main color beads and go down the next main color bead from the last row. Then pick up 2 size-11 accent beads and go up through the next main color bead. Repeat until there are 7 sets of 2 main color beads with 2 size-11 accent beads (a total of 14 beads) between each set.

Flower pattern 6
The working thread should now be coming out of one of the first main color beads of a set. Pick up 3 size-15 accent beads and then go down the next main color bead. This will create a picot. Then weave over to the next set of main color beads and repeat. Keep repeating until there is a picot on each set of main color beads. End with the working thread coming out of the third main color bead of the flat herringbone counting down from the outside edge.

Flower pattern 7
Pick up 1 size-11 accent bead and go up through the third main color bead of the next set of 2 beads. This bead will sit on top of the herringbone base. Pick up 1 more size-11 accent bead and go down the next main color bead (it will always be the third bead counting down from the outside edge). Keep adding beads this way until there are 14 size-11 accent beads added to the top of the herringbone base. They will be slightly offset from each other. End with the working thread coming out of the first accent bead added in this row.

Flower pattern 8
Pick up 3 of the size-15 accent beads and go through the next size-11 accent bead from the last row. This will make a little point of beads. Keep repeating until there are 14 points in this row.

Flower pattern 9
Weave the working thread down and come out of one of the beads added in row 2 of flower pattern step 1. Pick up 1 size-11 accent bead and go through the next bead from that row. Keep repeating until there are 7 of the size-11 accent beads in this row. End with the working thread coming out of the first size-11 accent bead added in this row.

Flower pattern 10
Pick up 5 size-15 accent beads and go through the next size-11 accent bead from the last row. Keep repeating until there are 7 sets of size-15 accent beads in this row. End with the working thread coming out of a bead of the first row (the original circle of beads in flower pattern step 1).

Flower pattern 11
Pick up a 5mm crystal and go through a bead of the original circle across from where the working thread exited. This will make the crystal sit in the center of the flower. Reinforce one more time. Weave in and tie off the tail thread but leave the working thread attached. This completes 1 flower.

Make 19 more flowers following flower pattern steps 1–11. You need 20 flowers for the necklace. The flowers will be connected together to make them double-sided, so this will result in 10 double flowers for the necklace.

Assembly 1

The flowers are connected together with circle stitches (see page 10). Weave a working thread on one of the flowers so that it is coming out of the middle size-15 accent bead at a tip of the flower. Then go through the middle size-15 accent bead of another flower. Then go back through the accent bead the thread originally exited from on the opposite side. This is a circle stitch.

Assembly 2

Weave through the beads and come out of a set of size-11 accent beads added in flower pattern step 5. Use a circle stitch to sew them together to the set of size-11 accent beads of the other flower. Circle stitch all 7 flower tips and all 7 sets of accent beads between them together. Repeat with the other flowers. There should now be 10 double-sided flowers.

Assembly 3

Now the flowers need to be connected together. Circle stitches are used to make all the connections. Use the working threads that are left on the flowers. The connections are made either at the tip of the flowers or at the 2 accent beads between the flowers. The center of the necklace has 6 of the double flowers connected together with a 5mm crystal between each flower. The two middle flowers are connected together at the size-15 accent bead points. Then the next flowers on each side are connected at the 2 size-11 accent beads of the middle flowers and the size-15 accent bead point on the new flowers with a 5mm crystal. Then repeat the connections one more time to add another flower to each side. Now there should be 6 flowers connected together.

The photo shows the middle flower connection and one flower connection on the other side.

Assembly 4

Now 5 of the 8mm round beads need to be added to each side with another flower. The flower is added to the fifth 8mm bead at one of the size-15 accent bead points. Do not add a 5mm crystal before and after the 8mm beads. Reinforce through the 8mm beads as many times as the beads will allow. Repeat one more time to add 5 more 8mm beads and another flower on each side.

Closure pattern 1

Start a new thread approximately 1½ yards (1.4m) long, single thickness with no knot. Pick up 1 size-11 accent bead and turn it into a stop bead by going back through it from the tail end. Leave a 4" to 6" (10cm to 15cm) tail. Pick up 13 more size-11 accent beads for a total of 14 beads. Then pick up 1 more size-11 accent bead, skip the fourteenth bead and go back up the thirteenth size-11 accent bead. This will make the last 2 beads sit side by side. Pick up 1 size-11 accent bead, skip over a bead and go through the next bead (flat round peyote stitch; see page 17). Keep repeating to the end of the row.

Closure pattern 2

Pick up 1 size-11 accent bead and go down the next bead that is sticking out. Repeat to the end of the row. Keep adding rows this way until there are 4 beads at each end.

Closure pattern 3

Fold the piece in half. The working thread should be coming out of the end bead. Zip the sides together by going through the beads that stick out on each side, alternating back and forth. The tail thread and working thread should end up at the same end of the tube. Weave the tail thread in by going down the bead next to it that has the working thread coming out of it. Weave the tail thread in and tie it off. Then go through the tube with the thread so that it is coming out of the other end. Pick up a 5mm crystal and 3 size-15 accent beads. Skip the 3 size-15 accent beads and go back through the 5mm crystal and the tube. Pick up a 5mm crystal and 3 size-15 accent beads. Skip the 3 size-15 accent beads and go back through the crystal. Reinforce. Tie off the working thread. This completes the toggle bar.

Closure pattern 4

Weave the working thread on the last flower on the necklace so that it is coming out of the set of size-11 accent beads between the points across from the connection to the 8mm beads. Pick up 10 size-11 accent beads and go through the seventh and eighth beads of the peyote tube, counting over from one end. Then pick up 10 more size-11 accent beads and go through the accent beads of the flower that the thread originally exited from on the opposite side. Reinforce.

Closure pattern 5

Weave a working thread on the end flower on the other side so that it is coming out of the set of size-11 accent beads between the points across from the connection to the 8mm beads. Then pick up 26 size-11 accent beads and go back through the size-11 accent beads the thread originally exited from on the opposite side.

Closure pattern 6

Pick up 1 size-11 accent bead, skip the first size-11 accent bead of the circle and go through the second size-11 accent bead of the 26. Skip the next accent bead and go through the next one (flat round peyote stitch; see page 17). Repeat all the way around the circle. This completes the toggle circle. Tie off any remaining threads.

Bracelet

Bracelet pattern 1

Follow flower pattern steps 1–11 and assembly steps 1–2 of the necklace to make 4 double-sided flowers. Then use circle stitches (see page 10) to connect the flowers. The connections are made either at the tip of the flowers or at the 2 accent beads between the flowers. There are 3 flowers on one side of the bracelet and 1 flower after the 8mm beads. The photo shows the connections to the 3 flowers. The 3 flowers have a 5mm crystal between them that is added with the circle stitch.

Bracelet pattern 2

On the third flower, weave the working thread so that it is coming out of the 2 accent beads across from the point where it is connected to the other flowers. Then pick up 9 of the 8mm beads and go through the point bead of the fourth flower. Reinforce as many times as the beads will allow.

Then follow closure pattern steps 1–3 to make a toggle bar and closure pattern steps 4–6 to connect the toggle bar and make a toggle circle at the other end. The toggle circle should be connected to the point of the last flower on the end with the 3 flowers. The toggle bar is connected to the single flower at the 2 accent beads between the points.

Cameo Necklace

I have always liked cameos.
They are romantic and elegant.
This necklace features one
as the main focal point. If
cameos aren't your thing, any
cabochon would work for this
design. A smaller cabochon
could also be used.

 **DIFFICULTY LEVEL**

Materials

Size 12 beading needle

Size D Nymo beading thread or FireLine

Small piece of heavy interfacing
or Lacy's Stiff Stuff

Small piece of black ultrasuede

E-6000 or similar adhesive

40mm x 30mm cameo

20mm x 9mm teardrop bead (Black)

8mm round bead for clasp (Black)

4 grams size-11 Japanese seed beads
for main color (Black)

12 grams size-15 Japanese seed beads
for main color (Black)

4 grams size-15 Japanese seed beads
for accent color (Silver-Lined Silver)

Cameo 1

Glue the cameo in the center of a piece of interfacing or Lacy's Stiff Stuff with an adhesive such as E-6000. The interfacing should be larger than the cabochon so there is room to add the beading. Start a thread approximately 2½ yards (2.3m) long, single thickness with a knot at the end. Bring the needle and thread up through the interfacing at the edge of the cameo to the top side. Pick up 3 size-11 main color beads, lay them along the cameo and go down at the end of them. Come back up through the interfacing at the beginning of the beads and go through all 3 beads again.

Pick up 3 more size-11 main color beads, lay them along the cameo in line with the first 3 beads and go down at the end of them. Then come back up and go through the last bead in the previous group and the 3 beads just added. Continue until there is an even number of beads sewn all the way around the cameo (this row is the backstitch row). **Note:** This row must have an even number of beads.

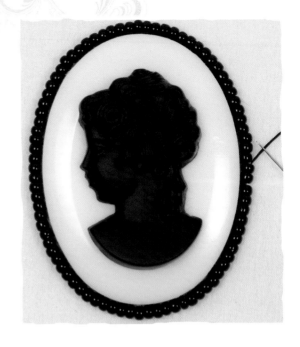

Cameo 2

The thread should be coming out of one of the size-11 main color beads. Pick up 1 size-11 main color bead, skip over the next bead in the original row and go through the next one. Repeat all the way around the cameo. This row will not look very uniform. After the last bead is added, also go up through the first size-11 main color bead of this row. This lines up the thread for the next row.

Cameo 3

This row will pull the beads in and make the bezel look nice and neat. Pick up 1 size-11 main color bead and go through the next size-11 bead from the last row. Repeat all the way around the cameo. Be sure to pull this row snug. After completing the row, weave the thread down and come out on the back of the interfacing.

Cameo 4

Trim away the excess interfacing as close to the beads as possible, being very careful not to cut any threads underneath the beadwork. Put a thin layer of glue on the back. Then place the beadwork onto the ultrasuede and press lightly. Let this dry for a bit, then trim the ultrasuede to match the interfacing. Weave the working thread so that it is coming out at the edge of the suede. Pick up 3 size-15 main color beads, and then go through the suede about a bead's width over from where the thread originally exited. Then go back up the third bead from the bottom up, forming a little picot.

Cameo 5

Pick up 2 size-15 main color beads and go through the suede about a bead's width over from where the thread originally exited, and then go back up the second bead. This will make a picot that sits on top of the previous picot. Repeat all the way around the cameo. For the last picot, only 1 bead is needed because it will be connected at the first bead of the edging. Pick up 1 size-15 main color bead, then go down the first bead of the edging, catch the suede and go back up the first bead. Set the cameo aside for now.

Chain pattern 1

Start a new thread, approximately 2½ yards (2.3m) long, single thickness with no knot. Pick up 1 accent bead, 3 size-15 main color beads, 1 accent bead and 3 more size-15 main color beads. Go back through the first accent bead, the next 3 size-15 main color beads and the second accent bead again from the tail end. This will create a little circle. Leave an 8" to 12" (20cm to 30cm) tail.

Chain pattern 2

Pick up 3 size-15 main color beads, 1 accent bead and 3 more size-15 main color beads. Then go back through the accent bead the thread originally exited from on the opposite side, and also go through the first 3 size-15 main color beads and the accent bead just picked up. This will create another circle. Keep making circles until you have a total of 28.

Chain pattern 3

Now another row of circles will be connected to the first row. Weave the working thread so that it is coming out of the second size-15 main color bead of the first circle, working toward the beadwork. Then pick up 1 size-15 main color bead, 1 accent bead, 3 size-15 main color beads, 1 accent bead and 1 more size-15 main color bead. Go back through the size-15 main color bead the thread originally exited from on the opposite side, and also go through the first size-15 main color bead and the first accent bead just added.

Chain pattern 4

Pick up 3 size-15 main color beads, 1 accent bead and 1 size-15 main color bead. Then go down through the second main color bead of the next circle from the previous row. Pick up 1 size-15 main color bead and go through the accent bead from the previous circle, and also go through the next 3 size-15 main color beads and the accent bead just added.

Chain pattern 5

Pick up 1 size-15 main color bead and go up through the second size-15 main color bead of the next circle of the previous row.

Chain pattern 6

Pick up 1 size-15 main color bead, 1 accent bead and 3 size-15 main color beads. Then go through the accent bead from the previous circle and also through the next 3 size-15 main color beads and the accent bead just added.

Repeat chain pattern steps 4–6 until you reach the end of the chain.

Chain pattern 7

Now a third row of circles will be added to the chain. Weave the working thread so that it is coming out of the second bead of the first circle going away from the beadwork. Pick up 1 size-15 main color bead, 1 accent bead, 3 size-15 main color beads, 1 accent bead and 1 size-15 main color bead. Then go back through the size-15 main color bead the thread originally exited from on the opposite side. Weave the thread around and come out of the second accent bead just added.

Continue adding circles following the techniques in chain pattern steps 4–6 to the end of the chain.

Chain pattern 8

At the end of the chain (28 circles), keep adding circles following chain pattern step 2 until you have 46 circles (there will be 18 single circles). After adding the last circle, the working thread should be coming out of the size-15 accent bead. This will be the top chain of the necklace, which is a little shorter, so make sure this chain is on the top as it is attached to the cameo.

Pick up 3 size-15 main color beads and go through a size-15 main color bead on the edge of the cameo that sticks out on the edging about ½" (13mm) down from the top. Then pick up 3 more size-15 main color beads and go back through the accent bead the thread originally exited from on the opposite side.

Chain pattern 9

Now picots will be added to both sides of the single circles. Weave the working thread so that it is coming out of the middle (second) size-15 main color bead on one side of the last circle. Pick up 3 size-15 main color beads and then go back through the size-15 main color bead the thread originally exited from on the opposite side. This will make a picot that sits on top of the size-15 main color bead. Weave over to the middle bead on the other side of the circle, and repeat. Keep repeating, adding picots to all the single circles (19 circles, counting the connection to the cameo).

Chain pattern 10

Now weave the working thread over to the accent bead of the last circle on the third row of connected chains (completed in chain pattern step 7). Add 20 single circles to it following chain pattern 2. Then pick up 3 size-15 main color beads and go through the sixth size-15 main color bead that sticks out on the edge of the cameo, counting away from the first chain connection.

Pick up 3 size-15 main color beads and go back through the accent bead the thread originally exited from on the opposite side. Then follow chain pattern step 9 to add picots to all the single circles of this chain.

Repeat chain pattern steps 1–10 for the strap on the other side of the cameo. Make sure that the second side is lined up with the first.

Cameo accent

Weave the working thread on the cameo down to the bead on the edging that sticks out and is closest to the center. Then pick up 5 size-15 main color beads, 1 accent bead, the teardrop bead and 3 size-15 main color beads. Skip the last 3 size-15 main color beads and go back up the teardrop and the accent bead. Then pick up 5 more size-15 main color beads and go back through the edging bead the thread originally exited from on the opposite side.

Closure pattern 1

Now the 8mm round bead needs to be added for the clasp. Weave the tail thread left on the chain so that it is coming out of an accent bead of a last circle on the outside edge. Pick up 5 size-15 main color beads, 1 accent bead, the 8mm bead and 3 accent beads. Then skip the last 3 accent beads and go back through the 8mm bead and the next accent bead. Then pick up 5 size-15 main color beads and go through the accent bead on the last circle on the other outside edge. Reinforce.

Closure pattern 2

On the other end strap, weave the tail thread left on the chain so that it is coming out of the accent bead of the last circle on the outside end. Pick up 5 size-15 main color beads, 1 accent bead and then enough size-15 main color beads to fit comfortably but snugly around the 8mm bead. Go back through the accent bead, then pick up 5 more size-15 main color beads and go through the accent bead on the other side of the chain. Reinforce. Tie off any remaining threads.

Beadazzled Necklace and Bracelet

I have always used crystals in my designs, and over the years I have started to use them in smaller sizes. I had purchased some 2mm crystals and wanted to use them in a design, and this dazzler is what resulted. I absolutely love how they look mixed in with the seed beads. They add bling, but are also delicate.

 **DIFFICULTY LEVEL**

Necklace Materials

Size 12 beading needle

Size D Nymo beading thread or FireLine

(50) 3mm bicone crystals for main color (Fuchsia)

(28) 3mm bicone crystals for accent color (Dorado)

(28) 2mm round crystals (Fuchsia)

(4) 4mm round beads (Light Bronze)

8mm round bead (Light Bronze)

2 grams size-11 Japanese seed beads (Metallic Bronze)

7 grams size-15 Japanese seed beads
for main color (Metallic Bronze)

6 grams size-15 Japanese seed beads
for accent color (Silver Bronze Gold Luster)

Bracelet Materials

Size 12 beading needle

Size D Nymo beading thread or FireLine

(98) 3mm bicone crystals for main color (Fuchsia)

(42) 3mm bicone crystals for accent color (Dorado)

(42) 2mm round crystals (Fuchsia)

(3) 4mm round beads (Light Bronze)

6mm round bead (Light Bronze)

2 grams size-11 Japanese seed beads (Metallic Bronze)

3 grams size-15 Japanese seed beads
for main color (Metallic Bronze)

2 grams size-15 Japanese seed beads
for accent color (Silver Bronze Gold Luster)

Necklace

Medium circle 1

Start with 2½ yards (2.3m) of thread, single thickness with no knot. Pick up a 4mm bead and 7 size-15 accent beads. Go back through the 4mm bead on the opposite side from where the thread originally exited. Leave a 10" to 12" (25cm to 30cm) tail. Pick up 7 size-15 accent beads and go back through the 4mm bead on the opposite side from where the thread originally exited. Then go back through all 14 of the size-15 accent beads again and pull snug. This will make a circle of beads around the 4mm bead.

Pick up 1 size-15 accent bead and go back through the size-15 accent bead the thread originally exited from on the opposite side and also go forward through the next size-15 bead of the original circle. This will make the size-15 bead just added sit on top of the previous bead. Keep repeating until there are 14 size-15 accent beads sitting on top of the original circle of size-15 accent beads. End with the working thread coming out of one of the size-15 accent beads just added.

Medium circle 2

Weave the working thread through all 14 size-15 accent beads just added. Also go forward through the first bead again. Pull snug. This will make the beads sit on top of the original circle of size-15 accent beads.

Medium circle 3

The working thread should now be coming out of one of the size-15 accent beads. Pick up 1 size-15 accent bead and go back through the bead the thread originally exited from on the opposite side, and also go forward through the next size-15 accent bead. This will make the new bead sit on top of the previous bead. Repeat until there are 14 size-15 accent beads on top of the circle of beads. End with the working thread coming out of one of the top size-15 accent beads.

Medium circle 4

Pick up 1 size-15 main color bead and then go through the next size-15 accent bead. Keep repeating until there are 14 size-15 main color beads between the size-15 accent beads of the last row. End with the working thread coming out of a size-15 main color bead.

Medium circle 5

Pick up 1 size-15 main color bead and go back through the bead the thread originally exited from on the opposite side, and also go forward through the next accent bead and the next main color bead. Repeat until there are a total of 14 of the size-15 main color beads on top of the last row of size-15 main color beads.

Medium circle 6

Weave over to the other original circle of size-15 accent beads and repeat medium circle steps 3–5. This will give the circle two layers of beads. Weave the working thread so that it is coming out of one of the top size-15 main color beads of the last row. The two layers are going to be joined at this point. Go through the next main color bead of the other layer and then go through the next main color bead of the layer the thread originated in. Keep going back and forth through the main color beads of the 2 layers until they are all connected. Also go through the first bead again to close the circle more neatly. There should now be 28 main color beads on the outside row.

Medium circle 7

Pick up 3 size-15 accent beads, skip over the next main color bead and go through the next one. Repeat until there are 14 points around the circle. End with the working thread coming out of the middle size-15 accent bead of the first point added in this row.

Medium circle 8

Pick up 1 of the 3mm accent crystals and go through the middle bead of the next point. Repeat until there are 14 of the 3mm accent crystals between the points. End with the working thread coming out of one of the crystals.

Medium circle 9

Pick up 3 size-15 main color beads and go back through the 3mm crystal the thread originally exited from on the opposite side. This will create a picot on top of the crystal. Then pick up a 2mm crystal and go through the next 3mm crystal. Repeat until there is a picot over each 3mm crystal, and there are 14 of the 2mm crystals.

Medium circle 10

Put a needle on the tail thread left earlier. Weave it so that it is coming out of a size-15 main color bead from the first row of size-15 main color beads. Pick up 3 size-15 accent beads and then go through the next size-15 main color bead. This will create a point. Repeat until there are 14 points that stick out. This completes the medium circle. Tie off the tail thread but leave the working thread attached.

Make 2 smaller circles following medium circle steps 1–7. Tie off the tail threads but leave the working threads attached. Set them aside for now.

Large circle 1

To make the large circle, follow medium circle steps 1–6. Then pick up 1 size-15 main color bead and go back through the main color bead the thread originally exited from on the opposite side, and also go forward through the next main color bead. This will make the new size-15 main color bead sit on top of the main color bead of the previous row. Repeat until there are 28 size-15 main color beads in this row. End with the thread coming out of a size-15 main color bead on the row just added.

Large circle 2

Pick up 1 size-11 bead and go through the next 2 size-15 main color beads. Repeat until there are a total of 14 size-11 beads in this row. End with the thread coming out of the first size-11 bead added in this row.

Large circle 3

Pick up 3 size-15 accent beads and go through the next size-11 bead. This will create a point. Repeat until there are 14 points. End with the working thread coming out of the second size-15 accent bead of the first point added in this row.

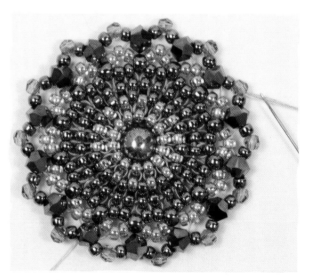

Large circle 4

Pick up a 3mm accent crystal and go through the second size-15 accent bead of the next point from the previous row. Repeat until there are 14 of the 3mm accent crystals. End with the working thread coming out of the first crystal added in this row.

Large circle 5

Pick up 1 size-15 main color bead, 1 of the 2mm crystals and 1 size-15 main color bead. Go through the next 3mm crystal from the previous row. Repeat until there are a total of 14 of the 2mm crystals with a size-15 main color bead on each side. End with the working thread coming out of the first 2mm crystal added in this row.

Large circle 6

Pick up 3 size-15 main color beads and go back through the 2mm crystal the thread originally exited from on the opposite side. This will make a point (or picot) over the 2mm crystal. Pick up 4 size-15 accent beads and go through the next 2mm crystal. Repeat until there is a picot over each 2mm bead with 4 size-15 accent beads in between. End with the working thread coming out of the second bead of the first 3 size-15 main color beads over the 2mm crystal.

Large circle 7

Pick up 2 size-15 accent beads, 1 of the 3mm main color crystals and 2 size-15 accent beads. Go through the second main color bead of the next picot over the next 2mm crystal. Repeat until there are 14 of the 3mm main color crystals in this row. End with the working thread coming out of the first 3mm main color crystal added in this row.

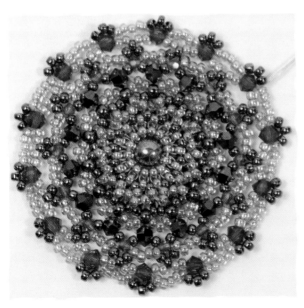

Large circle 8

Pick up 3 size-15 main color beads and go back through the 3mm main color crystal the thread originally exited from on the opposite side. This creates a picot over the crystal. Pick up 5 size-15 accent beads and go through the next 3mm main color crystal from the previous row. Repeat until there are picots over each 3mm main color crystal.

Then repeat medium circle step 10, except for the part about making the two smaller circles. This completes the large circle.

Large square 1
Start a new thread with approximately 2 yards (1.8m), single thickness with no knot. Pick up 4 of the 3mm main color crystals. Go back through all 4 crystals again from the tail end. Also go forward through the first crystal again to pull them closer together. Leave a 4" to 6" (10cm to 15cm) tail. Think of each unit of 4 crystals as a square.

Large square 2
Pick up 3 of the 3mm main color crystals and go back through the crystal the thread originally exited from on the opposite side, and also go forward through the first 2 crystals of the 3 just picked up. Repeat, except on the last part, go through only the first crystal of the 3 just picked up.

Large square 3
Pick up 3 of the 3mm main color crystals and go back through the crystal the thread originally exited from on the opposite side. Also go through the 3 crystals just picked up and then go through the crystal of the next square. This lines up the thread for the next square.

Large square 4
Pick up 2 of the 3mm main color crystals and go through the side crystal of the previous square and go back through the crystal the thread originally exited from on the opposite side. Also go through the first crystal of the 2 just picked up.

Large square 5
Pick up 2 of the 3mm main color crystals and go through the bottom crystal of the next square of the previous row and also go back through the crystal the thread exited from on the opposite side. Then go through the first crystal of the 2 just picked up.

Large square 6
Repeat large square steps 3-5 to add 1 more row.

Large square 7

The working thread should be coming out of a crystal at the end of a row. Pick up 1 size-11 bead and go through the next crystal. Repeat until there is a size-11 bead between each crystal on the outside edge. End with the working thread coming out of a size-11 bead on a corner.

Large square 8

Pick up 3 size-15 main color beads and go back through the size-11 bead the thread originally exited from on the opposite side. This will make a picot on top of the size-11 bead. Pick up 3 size-15 main color beads and go through the next size-11 bead. Keep adding 3 size-15 main color beads between the size-11 beads until you get to the corner opposite the corner you started in. Pick up 3 size-15 main color beads and go back through the size-11 bead the thread originally exited from on the opposite side. Then continue adding 3 size-15 main color beads between the remaining size-11 beads. There should only be a picot on 2 of the 4 corners.

Large square 9

Weave the working thread so that it is coming out of the crystal below the end crystal on the top. It should be the crystal where the hole of the crystal is lined up with the next crystal. Pick up 1 size-11 bead and go through the next crystal. Repeat one more time. Then go through the end crystal and the next crystal with the holes lined up. Pick up 1 size-11 bead and go through the next crystal. Repeat one more time. There should be 4 size-11 beads on top of the square.

Repeat on the other side of the square. There should be 4 size-11 beads on each side of the square. This completes the large square. Tie off the tail thread but leave the working thread attached.

Small square 1

Repeat large square step 1. Then pick up 3 of the 3mm main color crystals and go back through the crystal the thread originally exited from on the opposite side, and also go through the first crystal of the 3 just picked up.

Small square 2

Pick up 3 of the 3mm main color crystals and go through the crystal the thread originally exited from on the opposite side and also go through the 3 crystals just picked up. Then go through the bottom crystal of the first square.

Small square 3

Pick up 2 of the 3mm main color crystals and then go through the side crystal of the previous square, the bottom crystal the thread originally exited from and the first crystal of the 2 just picked up.

Small square 4

The working thread should be coming out of a crystal at the end of a row. Pick up 1 size-11 bead and go through the next crystal. Repeat until there is a size-11 bead between each crystal on the outside edge. End with the working thread coming out of a size-11 bead on a corner.

Small square 5

Pick up 3 size-15 main color beads and go back through the size-11 bead the thread originally exited from on the opposite side. This will make a picot on top of the size-11 bead. Pick up 3 size-15 main color beads and go through the next size-11 bead. Repeat, adding a picot to two more corners. On the last corner, do not add a picot over the size-11 bead.

Small square 6

Weave the working thread so that it is coming out of a crystal in the center of the square. Pick up 1 of the size-11 beads and go through the next crystal. The size-11 bead should sit in the center of the square. Repeat on the other side of the square. Tie off the tail thread but leave the working thread attached. This completes the small square.

Assembly 1

Weave the working thread of the large square so that it is coming out of the first 2 size-15 main color beads that are next to one of the corners without a picot over the size-11 bead. Then go through the middle bead of an outside point on the large circle. Weave through the circle and come out of the middle bead of the previous point. Then go through the previous 2 size-15 main color beads. Refer to the photo for the proper thread path. Weave in and tie off the working thread.

Assembly 2

Weave the working thread on the medium circle so that it is coming out of a second size-15 main bead on an outside point. Make sure the sides of the circles with the extra layer of points are on the same side. Go through the middle size-15 main color bead on the large square that is next to the size-11 corner bead with no picot (across from the connection to the large circle). Go back through the size-15 accent bead the thread originally exited from on the opposite side. This is a circle stitch (see page 10). Weave over and repeat this connection on the next set of beads.

Assembly 3

Repeat the circle stitch connections with the medium circle and the small square directly across from the large square and medium circle connections.

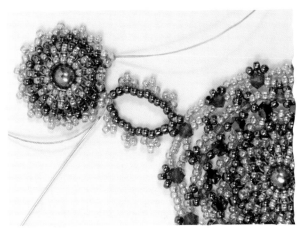

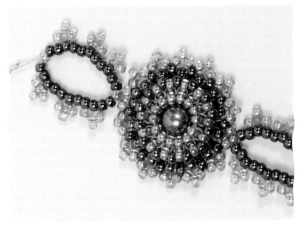

Strap section 1

Weave a working thread from one of the small circles so that it is coming out of the second size-15 accent bead of an outside point. Pick up 11 size-15 main color beads. Then go through the second size-15 main color bead at the fifth outside point up from the connection of the large circle and the large square. Then pick up 11 more size-15 main color beads and go back through the size-15 accent bead the thread originally exited from on the opposite side. Also go forward through the first 3 beads of the first 11 size-15 main color beads just picked up.

Then pick up 3 size-15 accent beads and go back through the size-15 main color bead the thread originally exited from on the opposite side. This will create a picot. Also go forward through the next 3 size-15 main color beads. Create 2 more picots on the first 11 size-15 main color beads and then create 3 more on the second set of 11 size-15 main color beads.

Strap section 2

Weave the working thread up to the second bead of the seventh point up from the connection to the large circle. Then pick up 11 size-15 main color beads, 1 size-15 accent bead and 11 size-15 main color beads. Go back through the point bead the thread originally exited from on the opposite side. Then add size-15 accent color picots to the circle, as described in strap section step 1. End with the working thread coming out of the size-15 accent bead.

Keep repeating, adding circles with picots to the strap until it is the desired length. A good average length is approximately 6" (15cm) long and has 14 circles.

Repeat strap section steps 1–2 for the second strap on the other side of the necklace. There should be 2 size-15 main color points on the outside row of the large circle between the two sides of the strap.

Closure pattern 1

The working thread should be coming out of the end size-15 accent bead of the last circle on a strap. Pick up 8 size-15 main color beads, 1 size-11 bead, the 8mm bead and 3 size-11 beads. Skip the 3 size-11 beads and go back through the 8mm bead and the next size-11 bead. Pick up 8 size-15 main color beads and go back through the size-15 accent bead the thread originally exited from on the opposite side. Reinforce.

Closure pattern 2

Weave the working thread on the other strap section so that it is coming out of the end size-15 accent bead of the last circle. Pick up enough size-15 main color beads to fit comfortably but snugly around the clasp bead. Go back through the size-15 accent bead the thread originally exited from on the opposite side. Reinforce. Tie off any remaining threads.

Bracelet

Bracelet pattern 1

Follow medium circle steps 1–9 of the necklace to make one circle. Tie off the tail thread but leave the working thread attached. Make 2 more circles. Then follow large square steps 1–9 of the necklace to make 4 crystal squares.

Weave a working thread so that it is coming out of a middle size-15 main color bead on an outside point of a circle. Pick up 1 size-15 main color bead and go through the size-11 bead of a square on a corner without a picot. Pick up 1 more size-15 main color bead and go back through the size-15 main color bead the thread originally exited from on the opposite side. Reinforce. Repeat with the other circles and squares until they are all connected. All the connections are directly across from each other.

Bracelet pattern 2

Weave a working thread so that it is coming out of the size-11 bead on the last square (the corner across from the connection, without the picot). Then pick up 11 size-15 main color beads, a 3mm main color crystal and 11 size-15 main color beads. Go back through the size-11 bead the thread originally exited from on the opposite side. Also go through the first 3 size-15 main color beads of the first group just picked up. Pick up 3 size-15 accent beads and go back through the size-15 main color bead the thread originally exited from on the opposite side. This will create a picot.

Bracelet pattern 3

Go through 3 more size-15 main color beads and make another picot with 3 size-15 accent beads. Repeat one more time. There should be 3 picots on the 11 size-15 main color beads. Weave through the remaining size-15 main color beads, go through the crystal and the first 3 size-15 main color beads of the next set of 11 beads and repeat, adding 3 more picots to the second set of 11 beads.

Bracelet pattern 4

Weave the working thread so that it is coming out of the 3mm crystal. Pick up 5 size-15 main color beads, the 6mm bead and 3 size-15 accent beads. Skip the last 3 size-15 accent beads and go back through the 6mm bead and the next main color bead. Pick up 4 size-15 main color beads and go back through the crystal on the opposite side from where the thread originally exited. Reinforce.

Bracelet pattern 5

Repeat bracelet pattern steps 2–4 on the other end of the bracelet, but instead of adding a clasp bead, add a loop of size-15 main color beads that fits comfortably but snugly around the clasp bead. Reinforce. Tie off any remaining threads.

Note: The bracelet is approximately 7½" (19cm) long. For a shorter bracelet, omit the decorative circles on each end. For a longer one, add more of the decorative circles on the ends.

Regency Necklace

The pendant on this eye-catching piece is made with bead embroidery. The strap is a gorgeous double-spiral rope, which also makes a beautiful bracelet.

DIFFICULTY LEVEL

Materials

Size 12 beading needle

Size D Nymo beading thread or FireLine

3 small pieces of heavy interfacing or Lacy's Stiff Stuff

3 small pieces of ultrasuede

E-6000 or similar adhesive

5mm bicone crystal (Light Colorado Topaz)

(70–80) 3mm pearls (Teal); amount used depends on spacing and tension

16mm x 6mm drop bead (Smoked Topaz)

8mm round bead for clasp (Dark Bronze)

27mm round crystal (Light Colorado Topaz)

(2) 18mm x 13mm rectangle crystals (Light Colorado Topaz)

5 grams size-15 Japanese seed beads for main color (Metallic Dark Bronze)

3 grams size-15 Japanese seed beads for accent color 1 (Teal Lined Iris)

3 grams size-15 Japanese seed beads for accent color 2 (Matte Lined Dark Topaz)

17 grams size-11 Japanese seed beads for color 1 (Metallic Dark Bronze)

14 grams size-11 Japanese seed beads for color 2 (Teal Lined Iris)

15 grams size-8 Japanese seed beads (Matte Teal Green Iris)

Round crystal 1

Glue the 27mm crystal in the center of a piece of interfacing or Lacy's Stiff Stuff with an adhesive such as E-6000. The interfacing should be larger than the crystal so there is room to add the beading.

Start a thread approximately 2½ yards (2.3m) long, single thickness with a knot at the end. Bring the needle and thread up through the interfacing at the edge of the crystal to the top side. Pick up 3 size-15 accent #2 beads, lay them along the crystal and go down at the end of them. Come back up through the interfacing at the beginning of the beads and go through all 3 beads again.

Pick up 3 more size-15 accent #2 beads, lay them along the crystal in line with the first 3 beads and go down at the end of them. Then come back up and go through the last bead in the previous group and the 3 beads just added.

Continue until there is an even number of beads that can be divided by 4 (such as 80 or 84) sewn all the way around the crystal (this row is the backstitch row). This will make the decreases in the later rows come out evenly.

Round crystal 2

The working thread should be coming out of one of the size-15 accent #2 beads. Pick up 1 size-15 accent #2 bead, skip over the next bead in the original row and go through the next one. Repeat all the way around the crystal. This is even=count tubular peyote. This row will not look very uniform. After the last bead is added, also go through the first size-15 accent #2 bead added in this row. This lines up the thread for the next row.

Round crystal 3

This row will pull the beads in and make the bezel look neater. Pick up 1 size-15 accent #2 bead and go through the next size-15 bead from the last row. Repeat all the way around the crystal. Be sure to pull this row snug. After the last bead is added, also go through the first size-15 accent #2 bead added in this row.

Round crystal 4

Pick up 1 size-15 main color bead and go through the next size-15 accent #2 bead from the last row. Repeat all the way around the crystal. After the last bead is added, also go through the first size-15 main color bead added in this row. This row will stick up a little and won't hug the crystal very closely, but be sure to pull the row snug.

Round crystal 5

Pick up 1 size-15 main color bead, then go through the next size-15 main color bead from the last row, through the next size-15 accent #2 bead from the row in round crystal step 3, and also through the next size-15 main color bead from the last row. Repeat all the way around the crystal. End with the working thread coming out of the first size-15 main color bead added in this row.

Round crystal 6

Pick up 2 size-15 accent #1 beads and then go through the next size-15 main color bead that was added in the last row. It should stick up. Repeat all the way around the crystal. End with the working thread coming out of the first 2 size-15 accent #1 beads added in this row. Be sure to pull this row snug. The beadwork should start to cup up around the crystal.

Round crystal 7

Pick up 1 size-15 main color bead and go through the next 2 size-15 accent #1 beads from the last row. Repeat all the way around the crystal. Then weave the working thread down through the beads and come out on the back of the interfacing.

Round crystal 8

Come back up to the front of the interfacing with the thread right next to the beaded bezel. Work a row of backstitch following round crystal step 1 with the size-11 color #1 beads. This is a decorative row, so it does not matter if it has an odd or an even number of beads.

Round crystal 10

Trim away the excess interfacing, getting as close to the beads as possible without cutting any of the threads underneath the beadwork. Put a thin layer of E-6000 or similar adhesive on the back of the piece with a toothpick. Then place the beadwork onto a piece of ultrasuede and press lightly. Let this dry and then trim the ultrasuede to match the interfacing. Then weave a working thread so that it is coming out at the edge of the ultrasuede.

Pick up 3 size-15 main color beads and then go through the suede about a bead's width over from where the thread originally exited. Then go back up the third bead just added from the bottom up. Pull snug. This will create a picot on the edge of the ultrasuede.

Round crystal 9

Work one more row of backstitch next to the row of size-11 color #1 beads, using the 3mm pearls with a size-15 main color in between each pearl. Watch the spacing at the end so that the pattern comes out evenly.

Round crystal 11

Pick up 2 size-15 main color beads and go through the ultrasuede about a bead's width over from where the last stitch was. Then go back up the second bead just picked up. The 2 beads just added will sit on the previous stitch and create another picot. Repeat all the way around the crystal. For the last stitch, pick up 1 size-15 main color bead and go down the first size-15 main color bead of the edging, catch the suede, and then come back up the same bead. This finishes the edging row.

Set this crystal aside for now with the working thread attached.

Rectangular crystal 1

Glue an 18mm x 13mm crystal to a piece of interfacing following round crystal step 1. Then work a row of backstitch around the crystal using size-15 accent #1 beads. **Note:** There needs to be an even number of beads that can be divided by 4 (such as 52 or 56) in this backstitch row.

Rectangular crystal 2

Work a row of tubular peyote with the size-15 accent #1 beads following round crystal step 2.

Rectangular crystal 3

Work another row of tubular peyote with the size-15 accent #1 beads following round crystal step 3.

Rectangular crystal 4

Pick up 1 size-15 main color bead and go through the size-15 accent #1 bead from the last row. Also go down through the next size-15 accent #1 bead from the previous row (rectangular crystal step 2) and the next size-15 accent #1 bead from the last row (rectangular crystal step 3). This row is a decrease. Repeat all the way around the crystal. After the last bead of the row is added, weave down through the beads and go through the interfacing.

Rectangular crystal 5

Come back up through the interfacing to the front side right next to the beaded bezel. Work a row of backstitch with the size-11 color #1 beads following rectangular crystal step 1. This row does not need to be an even number.

Rectangular crystal 6

Work one more row of backstitch next to the row of size-11 color #1 beads using the 3mm pearls with a size-15 main color bead in between each pearl. Watch the spacing at the end so that the pattern comes out evenly.

Rectangular crystal 7

Follow round crystal steps 10–11 to add the ultrasuede and the beaded edging to the crystal. Leave the working thread attached.

Repeat rectangular crystal steps 1–7 with another 18mm x 13mm crystal. There are 2 of these crystals on the necklace.

Connecting the crystals

On one of the rectangular crystals, find the 4 to 5 beads that stick out on the edging and are in the center on a short end. Weave the working thread so that it is coming out of the first bead of those center beads and go through a bead that sticks out on the edging of the round crystal. Then go through the next bead on the rectangular crystal that sticks out. Repeat until the beads are zipped together. Reinforce several times. **Note:** If your first attempt doesn't look centered, move over by a bead or try zipping another bead together until they do look centered.

Repeat with the other rectangular crystal on the other side of the round crystal.

Bead fringe

Weave a working thread on one of the rectangular crystals so that it is coming out of an edging bead that sticks out and is closest to the center of the bottom of the crystal. Then pick up 1 size-15 main color bead, a 5mm crystal, 1 size-15 main color bead, a drop bead, a 3mm pearl and 4 size-15 main color beads. Skip the last 3 size-15 main color beads and go back up the other beads. Go through the edging bead that the thread originally exited from on the opposite side. Tie off the working thread.

Bail pattern 1

Find the 5 edging beads that stick out and are the most centered at the top of the rectangular crystal that doesn't have the fringe. Then weave a working thread so that it is coming out of the first bead. Pick up 1 size-15 main color bead and go through the next edging bead that sticks up. Repeat 3 more times. The bail is 8 beads wide.

Bail pattern 2

Pick up 1 size-15 main color bead and go back through the bead from the last row that sticks out. Repeat to the end of the row. Keep adding rows until the bail is approximately 1¾" to 2" (4cm to 5cm) long. Then fold the bail over and sew the beads that stick out of the last row to the edging beads that stick out where the bail was started. They should fit together like a zipper. Tie off any remaining threads and set the pendant aside.

Rope pattern 1

Start a new thread approximately 2½ yards (2.3m) long, single thickness with no knot. Pick up 4 size-8 beads, 3 size-11 color #1 beads, 1 size-8 bead and 3 size-11 color #1 beads. Then go back through the first 4 size-8 beads just picked up. Leave a 10" to 12" (25cm to 30cm) tail.

Rope pattern 4

Now flip the entire piece of beadwork over so that the size-11 color #2 beads are on the left side. Then pick up 3 size-11 color #2 beads, 1 size-8 bead and 3 size-11 color #2 beads. Then go back through the last 4 size-8 core beads.

Now flip the beadwork over again so that the size-11 color #1 beads are on the left. Every time beads are added, they need to be added to the left side. Repeat rope pattern steps 3–4 until the rope is the desired length. The sample necklace is approximately 15" (38cm) long.

Rope pattern 2

Pick up 3 size-11 color #2 beads, 1 size-8 bead and 3 size-11 color #2 beads. Then go back through the original 4 size-8 beads. **Note:** The size-8 beads are the core of the spiral, and they will always be the beads you go back through.

Rope pattern 3

Pick up 1 size-8 bead, 3 size-11 color #1 beads, 1 size-8 bead and 3 size-11 color #1 beads. Then go back through the last 3 size-8 beads of the core and also go back through the first size-8 bead just picked up. Then push the beads added over to the left. Pull snug but not too tight.

Closure pattern 1

To add the clasp bead to the rope, the working thread should be coming out of the end size-8 core bead. Pick up 1 size-8 bead, 1 size-11 color #2 bead, 1 size-8 bead, the 8mm bead and 3 size-11 color #2 beads. Skip the last 3 size-11 color #2 beads and go back through the 8mm bead and the next size-8 bead. Pick up 1 size-11 color #2 bead and go back through the first size-8 bead picked up. Reinforce.

Closure pattern 2

Put a needle on the tail thread at the other end of the rope; it should be coming out of the end size-8 core bead. Pick up 1 size-8 bead, 1 size-11 color #2 bead, 1 size-8 bead and enough size-11 color #2 beads to fit comfortably but snugly around the clasp bead. Then go back through the last size-8 bead picked up. Pick up 1 size-11 color #2 bead and go back through the first size-8 bead picked up. Reinforce. Tie off any remaining threads and put the pendant on your rope.

Ribbon Lace Necklace and Bracelet

I named this necklace Ribbon Lace because the modified daisy chains used to create it reminded me of fabric ribbons. Using a matte bead in the design really makes the pattern stand out, but it also looks good with all shiny beads.

 **DIFFICULTY LEVEL**

Necklace Materials

Size 12 beading needle

Size D Nymo beading thread or FireLine

(38) 3mm pearls (Gold)

(8) 3mm bicone crystals for main color (Blue Zircon)

(4) 3mm bicone crystals for accent color (Crystal Dorado)

(3) 4mm bicone crystals (Blue Zircon)

(7) 9mm x 6mm smooth drop beads (Light Bronze)

8mm round bead (Light Bronze)

7 grams size-11 Japanese seed beads (Metallic Bronze)

8 grams size-15 Japanese seed beads for main color (Matte Teal AB)

2 grams size-15 Japanese seed beads for accent color (Cream)

Bracelet Materials

Size 12 beading needle

Size D Nymo beading thread or FireLine

(30) 3mm pearls (Gold)

(2) 4mm round beads (Light Bronze)

6 grams size-11 Japanese seed beads (Metallic Bronze)

8 grams size-15 Japanese seed beads for main color (Matte Teal AB)

2 grams size-15 Japanese seed beads for accent color (Cream)

Necklace

Center ribbon 1
Start with approximately 2½ yards (2.3m) of thread, single thickness with no knot. Pick up 1 size-11 bead and 2 size-15 main color beads. Repeat 3 more times. Then go back through all the beads again and also go forward through the first size-11 bead again to pull the circle closer together. Leave a 10" to 12" (25cm to 30cm) tail.

Center ribbon 2
Pick up 1 size-15 main color bead, 1 size-15 accent bead and 1 size-15 main color bead. Go back through the size-11 bead the thread originally exited from on the opposite side, and also go through the first size-15 main color bead and the size-15 accent bead just added.

Center ribbon 3
Pick up 1 size-15 main color bead and go through the size-11 bead across from the first size-11 bead.

Center ribbon 4
Pick up 1 size-15 main color bead and go back through the size-15 accent bead, the size-15 main color bead added in the previous step and the size-11 bead. This creates a little "x" in the middle of the circle.

Center ribbon 5
Pick up 2 size-15 main color beads and 1 size-11 bead. Repeat 2 more times. Pick up 2 size-15 main color beads after the last size-11 bead. Go through the size-11 bead the thread is exiting from on the opposite side.

Center ribbon 6
Repeat center ribbon steps 2–4. This will make 2 circles with x's in the middle. Then keep repeating center ribbon step 5 and center ribbon steps 2–4 to make a total of 12 circles with x's in the middle.

Center ribbon 7

Weave the working thread so that it is coming out of the size-11 bead on the side of the last circle. Pick up 2 size-15 main color beads and 1 size-11 bead. Repeat 2 more times and then pick up 2 size-15 main color beads. Go back through the size-11 bead the thread originally exited from on the opposite side, and also go through the other beads and come out of the third size-11 bead just picked up.

Center ribbon 8

Follow center ribbon steps 2–4 to add the "x" in the middle of the circle.

Center ribbon 9

Pick up 2 size-15 main color beads and go through the size-11 side bead of the previous circle.

Center ribbon 10

Pick up 2 size-15 main color beads, 1 size-11 bead, 2 size-15 main color beads, 1 size-11 bead and 2 size-15 main color beads. Go through the size-11 bead of the last circle created.

Center ribbon 11

Follow center ribbon steps 2–4 to add the "x" in the middle of the circle. Repeat center ribbon steps 9–11 until there are 12 new circles with x's that are connected to the original 12 circles. This will be the center of the necklace.

Short fringe

Weave the working thread so that it is coming out of the size-11 bead at the end of the row. Pick up 1 size-15 main color bead, 1 of the 3mm main color crystals, 1 size-15 main color bead, 1 of the 3mm pearls, 1 size-11 bead, a drop bead and 3 size-11 beads. Skip the last 3 size-11 beads and go back up the rest of the beads until you get to the first size-15 main color bead. Pick up 1 size-15 main color bead and go through the size-11 bead of the circle on the opposite side from where the thread originally exited. Weave the working thread in and tie it off.

Put the needle on the tail thread. It should be coming out of the size-11 bead at the end of the other row of circles. Repeat the fringe on this row of circles. Weave in and tie off the tail thread.

Pearl embellishment

Start a new thread, approximately 1½ yards (1.4m) long, single thickness with no knot. Weave it into the beadwork so that it is coming out of the first size-11 bead in the middle of the 2 rows of circles (the end without the fringe). Pick up a 3mm pearl and go through the next size-11 bead of the next circle. Repeat until you have added a total of 11 of the 3mm pearls down the center of the beadwork.

Long fringe

The working thread should now be coming out of the last size-11 bead between the circles. Pick up 5 size-15 main color beads, 1 size-11 bead, 1 of the 3mm accent crystals, 1 size-11 bead, 1 of the 4mm crystals, 1 size-11 bead, 1 of the 3mm pearls, 1 size-11 bead, 1 of the 3mm accent crystals, 1 size-11 bead, 1 drop bead, 1 of the 3mm main color crystals and 3 size-11 beads. Skip the last 3 size-11 beads and go back up the rest of the beads. Weave the working thread in and tie it off.

Large side ribbons

Make another row of circles with 8 circles following center ribbon steps 1–6, using about 1½ yards (1.4m) of thread. Leave a 10" to 12" (25cm to 30cm) tail. The working thread should end up coming out of the last size-11 bead of the last circle. Pick up 3 size-15 main color beads, 1 size-11 bead, 1 of the 3mm accent crystals, 1 size-11 bead, 1 of the 4mm crystals, 1 size-11 bead, 1 of the 3mm pearls, 1 size-11 bead, a drop bead, 1 of the 3mm main color crystals and 3 size-11 beads. Skip the last 3 size-11 beads and go back up the other beads until you get to the 3 size-15 main color beads at the top. Pick up 3 size-15 main color beads and go through the size-11 bead of the circle on the opposite side from where the thread originally exited. Tie off the working thread but leave the tail thread attached.

Make one more piece just like this with 8 circles and the fringe (there are 2 on the necklace).

Medium side ribbons

Make another row of circles with 6 circles following center ribbon steps 1–6, using about 1 yard (.9m) of thread. Leave a 10" to 12" (25cm to 30cm) tail. The working thread should end up coming out of the last size-11 bead of the last circle. Pick up 3 size-15 main color beads, 1 of the 3mm main color crystals, 1 size-15 main color bead, 1 of the 3mm pearls, 1 size-11 bead, a drop bead and 3 size-11 beads. Skip the 3 size-11 beads and go back up the other beads until you get to the 3 size-15 main color beads. Pick up 3 size-15 main color beads and go back through the size-11 bead of the circle that the thread originally exited from on the opposite side. Tie off the working thread but leave the tail thread attached.

Make one more piece just like this with 6 circles and the fringe (there are 2 on the necklace).

Small side ribbons and strap pieces

Make another row of circles with 4 circles following center ribbon steps 1–6, using about 1 yard (.9m) of thread or less. Leave a 4" to 6" (10cm to 15cm) tail. After the circles are completed, weave the tail thread in but leave the working thread attached. Make 5 more pieces with 4 circles. There are 6 of these pieces on the necklace. They do not have any fringe.

Now you need to make a row of circles for the strap section. A good approximate length is 6" (15cm) long and has 29 circles. Leave a 10" to 12" (25cm to 30cm) tail. If you are not sure how long you want the strap section to be, make enough circles to connect them to the other pieces and finish the strap section later. Make a total of 2 strap pieces for the necklace.

Assembly 1

The pieces are connected with circle stitches (see page 10). Start with the center piece and 1 of the 8-circle pieces. Weave the tail thread on the 8-circle piece so that it is coming out of the first size-11 bead on the side. Pick up 1 size-11 bead and go through the first size-11 bead on the side of the center piece. Pick up 1 size-11 bead and go through the size-11 bead the thread originally exited from on the opposite side. This is the circle stitch connection. Repeat 3 more times on the next 3 sets of size-11 beads. Weave in and tie off the tail thread.

Assembly 2

Refer to the photo for the proper connections for half of the necklace. After the first half is completed, repeat on the other half. Use the threads left earlier to make the circle stitch connections. Note that after the 8-bead row of circles is connected, the rows are one circle higher for each remaining connection.

Accent pearls and crystal

Start a new thread approximately 2 yards (1.8m) long, single thickness with no knot. Weave it into the beadwork and come out of the third size-11 accent bead on the side of the 6-circle row. Pick up a 3mm pearl and then go through the bottom size-11 accent bead of the circle stitch connection. The pearls are added from a size-11 accent of a circle to a size-11 accent bead of a connection. Refer to the photo for the proper placement of the pearls. At the top center, add a 3mm main crystal with a size-11 bead on each side instead of a pearl.

Closure pattern 1

Weave a working thread so that it is coming out of the last size-11 bead on the last circle of one of the strap sections. Pick up 4 size-11 beads, the 8mm bead and 3 size-11 beads. Skip the last 3 size-11 beads and go back through the 8mm bead and the next size-11 bead. Pick up 3 size-11 beads and go back through the size-11 bead the thread originally exited from on the opposite side. Reinforce.

Closure pattern 2

Weave a working thread on the other strap section so that it is coming out of the last size-11 bead on the last circle. Pick up enough size-11 beads to fit comfortably but snugly around the clasp bead. Go back through the size-11 bead the thread originally exited from on the opposite side. Reinforce. Tie off any remaining threads.

Bracelet

Bracelet pattern 1

Follow center ribbon steps 1–6 of the necklace until you have a row of circles long enough to fit around your wrist. A good average length is 7" (18cm), which has 31 circles.

Then follow center ribbon steps 7–11 until you have added a new row of circles with x's that are connected to the original row of circles. There should be 2 rows of circles connected side by side. Then weave the working thread so that it is coming out of the first size-11 bead in the middle of the 2 rows of circles.

Pick up a 3mm pearl and go through the next size-11 bead of the next circle. Repeat until there is a 3mm pearl between each size-11 bead down the center of the beadwork. End with the working thread coming out of the last size-11 bead between the circles. This is the center section of the bracelet.

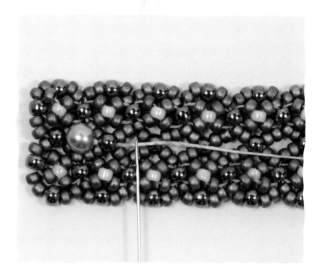

Bracelet pattern 2

Start a new thread approximately 2½ yards (2.3m) long, single thickness with no knot. Make another row of circles following center ribbon steps 1–6 of the necklace. This row should have the same amount of circles as the rows in the center section of the bracelet. Leave a 10" to 12" (25cm to 30cm) tail. Then make 1 more row of circles the same size (there are 2 single rows on the bracelet).

The pieces are connected with circle stitches (see page 10). Weave a working thread so that it is coming out of the first size-11 bead on the side of one of the single rows of circles. Pick up 1 size-11 bead and go through the first size-11 bead on the side of the center section. Pick up 1 size-11 bead and go back through the size-11 bead the thread originally exited from on the opposite side. This is a circle stitch connection. Weave down to the next size-11 bead on the side and repeat the circle stitch connection. Repeat until the chains are connected at every size-11 bead on the side. Then repeat with the second single row of circles on the other side.

Bracelet pattern 3

Weave a working thread so that it is coming out of the end size-11 bead of one of the circle connections. Pick up 6 size-15 main color beads, a 4mm bead and 3 size-15 main color beads. Skip the last 3 size-15 main color beads and go back through the 4mm bead and the next size-15 main color bead. Pick up 5 size-15 main color beads and go through the size-11 bead the thread originally exited from on the opposite side. Reinforce. Repeat on the other end size-11 bead of the other circle connection.

Bracelet pattern 4

Weave a working thread on the other end of the bracelet so that it is coming out of the end size-11 bead of a circle connection. Pick up enough size-15 main color beads to fit comfortably but snugly around the clasp bead. Go back through the size-11 bead the thread originally exited from on the opposite side. Reinforce. Repeat on the other end size-11 bead of the other circle connection. Tie off any remaining threads.

Circular Paths Necklace and Earrings

This intermediate project takes a little time but is well worth the effort. Another design option would be to omit the center section with the crystal rivolis and do a necklace with just the circles.

 **DIFFICULTY LEVEL**

Necklace Materials

Size 12 beading needle

Size D Nymo beading thread or FireLine

(2) 12mm crystal rivolis (Light Amethyst)

(12) 3mm tiny drop beads (Matte Gold)

(304) 3mm glass pearls (Burgundy)

(12) 3mm bicone crystals (Amethyst)

(3) 5mm bicone crystals (Amethyst)

16mm x 6mm drop bead (Purple Iris)

24 grams size-11 Japanese seed beads for main color (Matte Metallic Bronze Iris)

18 grams size-11 Japanese seed beads for accent color (Crystal/Gold Lined)

3 grams size-15 Japanese seed beads for main color (Metallic Iris Purple/Gold)

2 grams size-15 Japanese seed beads for accent color (Crystal/Gold Lined)

Earring Materials

Size 12 beading needle

Size D Nymo beading thread or FireLine

1 pair gold earwires

(2) 12mm crystal rivolis (Light Amethyst)

(4) 3mm glass pearls (Burgundy)

(16) 3mm bicone crystals (Amethyst)

(2) 5mm bicone crystals (Amethyst)

(2) 16mm x 6mm drop beads (Purple Iris)

1 gram size-11 Japanese seed beads for main color (Matte Metallic Bronze Iris)

2 grams size-15 Japanese seed beads for main color (Metallic Iris Purple/Gold)

1 gram size-15 Japanese seed beads for accent color (Crystal/Gold Lined)

Necklace

Circle pattern 1

Start with approximately 2½ yards (2.3m) of thread, single thickness with no knot. Pick up 4 size-11 main color beads and tie them into a circle. Leave a 4" to 6" (10cm to 15cm) tail. Go forward through one more bead to get away from the knot. Pick up 3 size-11 main color beads and go through the bead on the opposite side from where the thread is exiting, and also through the first 2 of the 3 beads just added. Repeat, for 21 circles total.

This technique is the first row of right-angle weave (see page 19). Think of each bead as a side of a square. As the base row is worked, the thread should always be exiting a side bead before you add a new circle or square.

Circle pattern 2

Now the strip of 21 circles needs to be joined together. The working thread should be exiting the end side bead. Pick up a size-11 main color bead and then go through the side bead on the other end of the strip. Make sure that the strip of beadwork is not twisted. Pick up a size-11 main color bead and go back through the side bead the thread originally exited from on the opposite side. Pull snug. Weave in and tie off the tail thread.

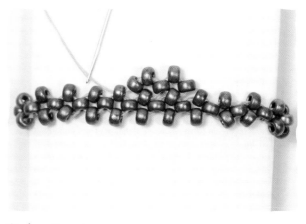

Circle pattern 3

Weave the working thread so that it is exiting from a top bead of a square. Then pick up 3 size-11 main color beads and go back through the bead the thread originally exited from on the opposite side. Then go through the first bead of the 3 just picked up.

Circle pattern 4

For the rest of the row, only 2 beads need to be picked up at a time (for right-angle weave). Pick up 2 size-11 main color beads and go through the top bead of the next square from the previous row on the far side, and also go through the side bead of the first square created in this row. Also go through the 2 beads just added and the top bead of the next square.

Circle pattern 5

Pick up 2 size-11 main color beads and go through the side bead of the last square, and also back through the top bead of the square from the previous row. Also go up the side bead of the square that was just created.

Keep adding squares by repeating circle pattern steps 4-5. The squares will alternate between the two stitch patterns. Repeat to the end of the row.

Circle pattern 6

To finish the row, on the last square, pick up a size-11 main color bead and go through the side of the first square of this row, the top bead of the previous row and the side bead the thread originally exited from on the opposite side. Also go through the size-11 main color bead just added. Pull snug.

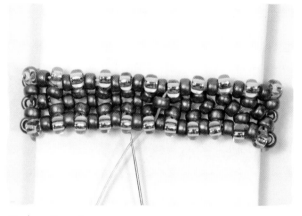

Circle pattern 7

The working thread should now be coming out of a top bead of a square. Pick up a size-11 accent bead and then go through the next top bead of the next square. Repeat this step all the way around the circle. When the top edge is done, weave down to the other side and repeat on the bottom edge.

Circle pattern 8

Now pinch the circle so that the size-11 accent beads meet and a channel is created by the two rows of right-angle weave. The working thread should be coming out of an accent bead on one side of the circle. Pick up a size-11 main color bead and go through the next accent bead on the other side of the circle that is at an angle, not directly across. The thread path forms a zigzag pattern around the circle. Be sure to pull the stitches snug. This row pulls the channel together and closes it up. Repeat all the way around the circle.

After adding the last bead, weave through several beads of the circle to help hold the beads in place. End with the working thread coming out of a main color bead in the middle of the channel.

Circle pattern 9

Pick up a 3mm pearl and go through the next main color bead of the channel. Repeat all the way around the circle (22 pearls total). End with the working thread coming out of a 3mm pearl. This row might start to ruffle a bit.

Circle pattern 10

Pick up a size-11 accent bead and go through the next 3mm pearl. Continue all the way around the circle. End with the thread coming out of a size-11 accent bead.

Circle pattern 11

Pick up 3 size-11 accent beads and go through the accent bead from the last row. Repeat all the way around the circle. This row will create little points. This completes one circle.

There are a total of 12 circles on this necklace, which is approximately 17½" (44cm) long. Adjust the number of circles accordingly for a longer or shorter necklace.

Large rivoli piece 1

Start a new thread, approximately 2 yards (1.8m) long, single thickness with no knot. Pick up 12 size-15 main color beads and go back through them from the tail end. Also go forward through 1 more bead to pull the circle closer together. Leave a 10" to 12" (25cm to 30cm) tail. Pick up 3 size-15 main color beads, skip the next bead of the original circle, and go through the next size-15 main color bead of the original circle. This will form a small point. Repeat all the way around the circle, for a total of 6 points. After adding the last point, also go through the first 2 beads of the first point of this row.

Large rivoli piece 2

Pick up 5 size-15 main color beads and go through the middle (second) bead of the next point from the last row. Repeat all the way around the circle. After adding the last point, also go through the first 3 beads of the first point of this row.

Large rivoli piece 3

Pick up 7 size-15 main color beads and go through the middle (third) bead of the next point from the last row. Repeat until you have gone all the way around the circle. After adding the last point, also go through the first 4 beads of the first point of this row.

Large rivoli piece 4

Pick up 5 size-15 main color beads and go through the middle (fourth) bead of the next point from the previous row. Pull snug. This row will make the beadwork cup up. Repeat all the way around the circle. Before adding the last point, insert a 12mm rivoli into the beadwork. Pull the beadwork snug around the crystal. After adding the last point, also go through the first 3 beads of the first point of this row.

Large rivoli piece 5

Pick up 3 size-15 main color beads and go through the middle (third) bead of the next point from the last row. Repeat all the way around the circle. Pull snug.

Large rivoli piece 6

Weave the working thread so that it is coming out of the middle (fourth) bead of the row of points with 7 beads per point. Pick up 3 size-15 accent beads and go back through the size-15 main color bead of the point on the opposite side from where the thread originally exited. Also go forward through the first 2 beads of the 3 size-15 accent beads just added. Then pick up 3 size-15 main color beads, one of the tiny drop beads and 3 size-15 main color beads. Then go back through the size-15 accent bead the thread originally exited from on the opposite side.

Large rivoli piece 7

Weave over to the middle (third) bead of the second row of points with 5 beads (the row added in large rivoli piece step 4), and repeat large rivoli piece step 6 to add another picot with a drop bead. Repeat large rivoli piece steps 6–7 until there are 12 picots with tiny drop beads around the circle. The picots will be slightly offset because of adding them to the two different rows.

Large rivoli piece 8

Weave the working thread so that it is coming out of the middle (second) bead of the last row of points with 3 beads per point (the row added in large rivoli piece step 5). Pick up 3 size-15 accent beads and then go back through the point bead the thread originally exited from on the opposite side. Weave over and come out of the middle (second) bead of the next point from large rivoli piece step 5 and repeat. Repeat for a total of 6 picots, one on each 3-bead point. End with the working thread coming out of the middle (second) bead of the last picot just added.

Large rivoli piece 9

Pick up one size-15 main color bead, one 3mm crystal and one size-15 main color bead. Then go through the middle (second) bead of the next picot created in the last row. Repeat to form 6 crystals around the circle. This row will stand up a little.

Large rivoli piece 10

Weave the working thread so that it is coming out of a 3mm crystal. Pick up 3 size-15 main color beads and go back through the crystal on the opposite side from where the thread originally exited. This will form a picot on top of the crystal. Weave over to the next crystal and repeat. Repeat until all 6 crystals have a picot over them. Weave in and tie off the working thread but leave the tail thread attached. Set this piece aside for now.

Small rivoli piece 1

Repeat large rivoli piece steps 1–5 with the other 12mm crystal rivoli. Then weave the working thread so that it is coming out of the second bead of a point from the 7-beads-per-point row. Pick up a size-11 main color bead, a 3mm crystal and a size-11 main color bead. Then go through the second bead on the other side of the point. Weave over to the next point from the 7-beads-per-point row, and repeat. Repeat until you have 6 picots with a 3mm crystal.

Small rivoli piece 2

Weave the working thread so that it is exiting the middle (fourth) bead of a point from the 7-beads-per-point row. Pick up 3 size-15 accent beads and go back through the size-15 main color bead the thread originally exited from on the opposite side. This will create a picot. Then weave over to the middle (third) bead of the next point from the second 5-beads-per-point row and repeat the picot. Repeat to make 12 picots around the circle that are slightly offset.

Small rivoli piece 3

Now weave the working thread so that it is coming out of the middle (second) bead of a point from the last 3-beads-per-point row. Pick up 3 size-15 accent beads and go back through the size-15 main color bead the thread originally exited from on the opposite side. This will create a picot. Repeat on the other middle beads on the 3-beads-per-point row, for 6 total picots.

Small rivoli piece 4

Weave the working thread so that it is coming out of a middle (third) bead of a point of the first 5-beads-per-point row. Pick up a 3mm pearl, a 5mm crystal, a 3mm pearl, the drop bead, a 3mm pearl and 3 size-15 accent beads. Skip the 3 accent beads and go back up the other beads. Go through the size-15 main color bead the thread originally exited from on the opposite side. This photo shows the crystal from the back. Tie off the tail and working threads.

Assembly 1

Center the large rivoli piece on top of a circle. Then weave the tail thread on the rivoli piece so that it is coming out of the middle (third) bead of a point from the first 5-beads-per-point row. Go through a size-11 main color bead on the inside of the circle and back through the bead the thread originally exited from on the opposite side. This is a circle stitch (see page 10). Weave over to the next middle bead of the next point from the 5-beads-per-point row and repeat. Repeat all the way around the row.

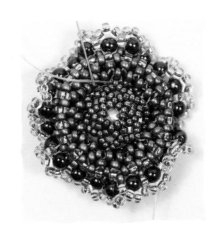

Assembly 2

Now, attach the small rivoli piece to the large one. Weave a working thread from the circle that has the large rivoli piece attached to it so that the thread is coming out of the middle (second) accent bead of the last row of points. Pick up a size-11 main color bead, a 3mm pearl and a size-11 main color bead. Go through the third 3mm crystal (counting up from the fringe) of the picot on the small crystal piece. Then weave over to the middle (third) bead of the first 5-beads-per-point row.

Pick up a 3mm pearl and go through the middle (second) accent bead of the next point on the original circle, then go back through the 3mm pearl and the main color bead of the crystal piece on the opposite side from where the thread originally exited (a circle stitch, see page 10). Weave over to the next 3mm crystal. Pick up a size-11 main color bead, a 3mm pearl and a size-11 main color bead. Then go through the middle (second) accent bead of the next point of the circle. Weave the thread in and tie it off.

Toggle bar pattern 1

Start a new thread, approximately 1 yard (.9m) long, single thickness with no knot. Pick up one size-11 main color bead and turn it into a stop bead by going back through it from the tail end. Leave a 4" to 6" (10cm to 15cm) tail. Pick up 17 more size-11 main color beads for a total of 18. Then pick up one more size-11 main color bead, skip the eighteenth bead and go up the seventeenth. This will make the last 2 beads sit side by side. Then pick up one size-11 main color bead, skip over the next bead and go through the next one. Repeat to the end of the row. The working thread should end up coming out of the first bead.

Toggle bar pattern 2

Pick up a size-11 main color bead and go down the bead that is sticking out (the last bead from the last row). Repeat to the end of the row. Keep adding rows this way until you have 5 beads along the top and bottom edge.

Toggle bar pattern 3

Fold the piece in half. The working thread should be coming out of an end bead. Zip the sides together by going through the beads that stick up on each side, alternating back and forth. The beads will fit together like a zipper. Both the tail thread and the working thread should now be at the top of the tube. Weave the tail thread in by going down the bead next to it (the one with the working thread exiting from it). This will connect the beads at the top. Weave the tail thread in and tie it off.

The working thread should be coming out of a bead at the end of the tube. Go through the tube with the thread. Then pick up a 5mm crystal and 3 size-11 accent beads. Skip the 3 size-11 accent beads and go back through the 5mm crystal and the tube. Pick up a 5mm crystal and 3 size-11 accent beads, skip the size-11 accent beads and go back down the 5mm crystal. Reinforce. Weave the working thread in and tie it off.

Assembly 3

Weave a working thread on a circle so that it is coming out of a middle (second) size-11 accent bead on the last row of points. Pick up a 3mm pearl and then go through the middle size-11 accent bead of the center circle at the sixth point up from where the small crystal rivoli piece is attached. Then go back through the 3mm pearl and the size-11 accent bead the thread originally exited from on the opposite side. This is a circle stitch (see page 10) and is used to connect all the circles together.

Assembly 4

This photo shows the placement for the center piece and the other circles. Use circle stitches and the 3mm pearls for all the connections. There are 3 of the 3mm pearls connecting each circle, and there are 8 points on the circles on each side of the connections. The connections are directly across from each other. One of the circles is used for the toggle bar, so one side of the necklace will have an extra circle.

Assembly 5

The toggle bar is connected to the side of the necklace with one less circle. There should be 9 points on the last row of the circle on each side of the connection. Weave the working thread on the circle so that it is coming out of the middle bead of the tenth point from the circle connection. Pick up a 3mm pearl and 10 size-11 main color beads, then go though the ninth and tenth bead on the toggle bar. Pick up 10 size-11 main color beads and go back through the 3mm pearl and the size-11 accent bead the thread originally exited from on the opposite side. Reinforce. Tie off any remaining threads.

Earrings

Earring pattern 1

Follow small rivoli piece steps 1–3 of the necklace to make and embellish a crystal rivoli bezel. Then weave the working thread so that it is coming out of a 3mm crystal. Pick up 5 size-15 main color beads, a size-15 accent bead, a 3mm crystal, a size-15 accent bead, a 5mm crystal, a size-15 accent bead, a 3mm crystal, a size-11 main color bead, a 3mm pearl, a size-11 main color bead, a drop bead, a 3mm pearl and 3 size-15 accent beads. Skip the last 3 size-15 accent beads and go back up the remaining beads until you reach the first size-15 accent bead. Then pick up 5 size-15 main color beads and go through the 3mm crystal the thread originally exited from on the opposite side.

Earring pattern 2

Weave the working thread up to the 3mm crystal across from the fringe. Pick up 10 size-15 main color beads and one of the earwires. Then go back through the 3mm crystal on the opposite side from where the thread originally exited. Reinforce.

Repeat these steps for the other earring.

Tie off any remaining threads.

Coming Up Roses Lariat

I love flowers, nature motifs and fringe, so I combined them in this lariat. The herringbone chain would also look great in black, with purple or red roses.

DIFFICULTY LEVEL

Materials

Size 12 beading needle

Size D Nymo beading thread or FireLine

(3) 9mm x 6mm crystal drop beads (Rose)

20 grams size-11 Japanese cylinder beads for main color (Metallic Green Iris)

3 grams size-11 Japanese seed beads for accent color (Burgundy Gold Luster)

11 grams size-15 Japanese seed beads for main color (Metallic Green Iris)

6 grams size-15 Japanese seed beads for accent color (Burgundy Gold Luster)

Chain pattern 1

Start with approximately 2½ yards (2.3m) of thread, single thickness with no knot. Pick up 2 size-11 main color beads and go back through them from the tail end. They should sit side by side. Leave a 10" to 12" (25cm to 30cm) tail. Pick up 1 size-11 main color bead and go back through the last bead added on the opposite side from where the thread originally exited, and also go through the bead just picked up. This will make the new bead sit next to the other beads. Keep adding beads this way until there are a total of 6 size-11 main color beads.

Chain pattern 2

Pick up 2 size-11 main color beads and go down the second bead of the first row and come up the third bead. Pick up 2 size-11 main color beads and go down the fourth bead of the first row and come up the fifth bead. Pick up 2 size-11 main color beads and go down the sixth bead of the first row. Pick up 1 size-15 main color bead and go up the second size-11 main color bead just added.

Chain pattern 3

Pick up 2 size-11 main color beads and go down the next size-11 main color bead from the last row and up the next one. Repeat 2 more times (flat herringbone stitch; see page 15). On the third stitch, after going down the last size-11 main color bead from the last row, pick up 1 size-15 main color bead and then go up the last size-11 main color bead just added. Repeat until the herringbone chain is the desired length. The herringbone chain on the sample necklace (not including the fringe) is approximately 23" (58cm) long.

Loop pattern 1

Weave the tail thread left on the chain at the beginning so that it is coming out of an end bead of the 6-bead row from chain pattern step 1. Pick up 35 size-11 main color beads and then go through the other end bead of the same 6-bead row. Then go through the second bead of the 6 and also go through the first bead of the 35 just added. Then pick up 1 size-11 main color bead, skip over the next bead and go through the next one. Repeat to the end of the row. After adding the last size-11 main color bead, go through the second bead of the 6 beads from chain pattern step 1 on this end.

Loop pattern 2

Go back through the end bead on the 6-bead row from chain pattern step 1 and also go through the first 2 beads on the loop. Then pick up 3 size-15 main color beads and go through the bead that sticks up from the last row. Repeat to the end of the loop. Then go through the first bead of the loop and the end bead of the 6-bead row from chain pattern step 1. This row might ruffle a bit. Tie off the tail thread.

Rose pattern 1

Start a new thread, approximately 2½ yards (2.3m) long, single thickness with no knot. Pick up 3 size-11 accent beads. Go back through all 3 of them again from the tail end. Also go forward through the first bead again. This will form a triangle. Leave a 10" to 12" (25cm to 30cm) tail.

Rose pattern 2

Pick up 7 size-15 main color beads, then skip the last bead picked up and go back through the next bead. Pick up 5 more size-15 main color beads and go through the next size-11 accent bead. Repeat 2 more times between the size-11 accent beads for a total of 3 leaves.

Rose pattern 3

The working thread should be coming out of a size-11 accent bead. Pick up 3 size-15 accent beads and then go through the next size-11 accent bead. This will make a small picot. Repeat 2 more times. After adding the third picot, also go through the first 2 beads of the first picot added in this row.

Rose pattern 4

Pick up 5 size-15 accent beads and go through the middle (second) bead of the next picot from the last row. Repeat 2 more times. After adding the last picot of this row, also go through the first 3 beads of the first picot added in this row.

Rose pattern 5

Pick up 7 size-15 accent beads and go through the middle (third) bead of the next picot from the last row. Repeat 2 more times. After adding the last picot, weave down and come out of one of the size-11 accent beads of the original triangle.

Rose pattern 6

Pick up 12 size-15 main color beads and 3 size-11 accent beads. Then go back through all 3 of the size-11 accent beads again to form a triangle. Also go forward through the first size-11 accent bead again.

Assembly 1

Follow rose pattern steps 2–6 to make 4 more roses for a total of 5 that are connected together. Now the roses need to be attached to the herringbone chain at the loop end. There isn't a specific thread path for this; the roses are tacked to the chain by going through a bead on the chain and then through a bead on the leaves or roses. Use the tail thread and working thread on the roses to do this. Slightly alternate the roses back and forth along the chain for a pleasing arrangement. Be sure to tack the roses down in enough places so that they are secure. Tie off the tail and working thread on the roses.

Assembly 2

The working thread at the end of the herringbone chain should be coming out of an end size-11 main color bead on the last row. Pick up 1 size-15 main color bead and go down the next size-11 main color bead of the last row, and come up the next bead. Repeat 2 more times. Weave the working thread in and tie it off.

Rose fringe 1

Follow rose pattern steps 1–6 to make a fringe with 7 roses; however, after each rose, pick up 15 size-15 main color beads instead of 12.

After the last rose is completed, pick up 18 size-15 main color beads. Then skip the last bead and go back through the next one. Pick up 6 size-15 main color beads, skip over 6 beads of the 18 and go through the next bead. This will make a leaf.

Then pick up 6 size-15 main color beads and 4 size-11 accent beads. Skip the last 3 size-11 accent beads and go back through the first one. This will make a little flower bud. Repeat 2 more times for 2 more leaves and flower buds.

Rose fringe 2

Pick up 6 size-15 main color beads, 1 size-11 accent bead, a drop bead and 4 size-11 accent beads. Skip the last 3 size-11 accent beads and go back up the first size-11 accent bead. Weave the working thread in and tie it off. This completes 1 fringe.

Make one more fringe this size following rose fringe steps 1–2, and then make 1 fringe with 9 roses instead of 7, which will be the center fringe.

Rose fringe 3

Put a needle on the tail thread left on one of the 7-rose fringes. Then pick up 15 size-15 main color beads and go through one of the end size-15 main color beads added in assembly step 2. Pick up 15 more size-15 main color beads and go back through the size-11 accent bead of the fringe that the thread originally exited from on the opposite side. Reinforce once more.

Add the longest fringe with 9 roses to the middle size-15 main color bead added in assembly step 1, but add 18 size-15 main color beads instead of 15. Then add the last fringe with 7 roses to the other end size-15 main color bead added in assembly step 1 with 15 size-15 main color beads. Tie off any remaining threads.

Index

A
adhesives, 9, 11
anklet, 49-51

B
backing materials, 9
backstitch, 11
bead counts, 23
Beadazzled
    bracelet, 97, 106
    necklace, 97, 98-105
beading mats, 8
beads, 8-9
beeswax, 8
bezel, 11
bicone crystals, 9
bracelets
    Beadazzled, 97, 106
    Flower Garland, 85, 90
    Fringed, 53, 61
    Ribbon Lace, 115, 122-123
    Rivoli Flowers, 75-79
    Sequins in Symmetry, 39, 40-42
    Victorian Circles, 25, 30-31

C
cabochons, 9
Cameo Necklace, 90-95
chain patterns, 20, 50, 70, 93-95. See also rope patterns
chevron stitch, 13
circle patterns, 26-27, 40-41, 81-82, 98-101, 126-128
circle stitch, 10
Circular Paths
    earrings, 125, 134
    necklace, 125, 126-133
circular patterns, 26-27, 40-41, 81-82, 98-101, 126-128
clasp beads, 9
clear polish, 33

Coming Up Roses Lariat, 135-139
Crystal Flower Necklace, 62-67
crystal rivolis, 9, 64
crystals, 9, 97
Czech glass pearls, 9

D
delica beads, 9
diamond pattern, 71
difficulty levels, 23
double spiral rope, 14
Drop Anklet, 49-51
drop beads, 28, 43, 51, 72, 95, 134
druk beads, 9

E
earrings
    Circular Paths, 125, 134
    Mobile Earrings, 69, 73-74
    Sequins in Symmetry, 39, 43

F
fire polish beads, 9
flat herringbone, 15
flat round herringbone, 16
flat round peyote, 17
Flower Garland
    bracelet, 85, 90
    necklace, 85, 86-90
flowers, 34-37, 64-65, 76-78, 86-87
focal pieces, 9
fringe patterns, 57-59, 67, 111, 118, 138-139
Fringed
    bracelet, 53, 61
    pendant, 53, 54-60

G
glass pearls, 9
glue, 9, 11

H
half-hitch knots, 10
herringbone, 15, 16

I
interfacing, 9, 11

J
Japanese seed beads, 8

K
knots, 10

L
lariat, 135-139
lighting, 8
loops, 136

M
magnifiers, 8
Midnight Lace Necklace, 44-48
Mobile
    earrings, 69, 73-74
    necklace, 69, 70-73

N
necklaces
    Beadazzled, 97, 98-105
    Cameo, 90-95
    Circular Paths, 125, 126-133
    Crystal Flower, 62-67
    Flower Garland, 85, 86-90
    Midnight Lace, 44-48
    Mobile Necklace, 69, 70-73
    Regency, 107-113
    Ribbon Lace, 115, 116-121
    Ruffled Rings, 80-83
    Victorian Circles, 25, 26-29
needles, 8

O

odd-count tubular peyote, 18

P

pearls, 118, 121
pendants
    Fringed Pendant, 53, 54–60
    Picot Petals, 33, 34–38
peyote, 9, 11, 17, 18
Picot Petals
    pendant, 33, 34–38
    ring, 33, 38
plastic trays, 8
pliers, 8

R

rectangles, 54–57
Regency Necklace, 107–113
reinforcing, 10
Ribbon Lace
    bracelet, 115, 122–123
    necklace, 115, 116–121
right-angle weave, 19
ring, 33, 38
Rivoli Flowers Bracelet, 75–79
rivolis, 9, 129–131
rope patterns, 14, 18, 37, 63, 112
rose pattern, 137–139
Ruffled Rings Necklace, 80–83

S

seed beads, 8
Sequins in Symmetry
    bracelet, 39, 40–42
    earrings, 39, 43
skill levels, 23
squares, 19, 102–104
St. Petersburg chain, 20
stop beads, 10
suede, 8, 9
synthetic beeswax, 8

T

tail thread, 10
thread
    conditioners, 8
    types, 8
    working with, 10
toggle pattern, 132, 133
tubular peyote, 18
tubular picot netting, 21

V

Victorian Circles
    bracelet, 25, 30–31
    necklace, 25, 26–29

W

working thread, 10

About the Author

Kelly Wiese has been designing beadwork, primarily jewelry, for approximately sixteen years. She teaches nationally at various bead shows and other venues. In 2011, she was a designer of the year for a national beading magazine, and she is the author of *Beaded Allure: Beadweaving Patterns for 25 Romantic Projects* (North Light Books). She spends as much time as possible in her home studio in Fort Morgan, Colorado, working on new designs and keeping up with her online business, The Bead Parlor (www.beadparlor.com). Her three cats and three dogs keep her company as she works, although she finds they aren't very helpful when she needs an opinion on a new design.

www.fwmedia.com

17 16 15 14 13   5 4 3 2

DISTRIBUTED IN CANADA BY FRASER DIRECT
100 Armstrong Avenue
Georgetown, ON, Canada L7G 5S4
Tel: (905) 877-4411

DISTRIBUTED IN THE U.K. AND EUROPE BY F&W MEDIA INTERNATIONAL
Brunel House, Newton Abbot, Devon, TQ12 4PU, England
Tel: (+44) 1626 323200, Fax: (+44) 1626 323319
Email: enquiries@fwmedia.com

DISTRIBUTED IN AUSTRALIA BY CAPRICORN LINK
P.O. Box 704, S. Windsor NSW, 2756 Australia
Tel: (02) 4560 1600, Fax: (02) 4577 5288
Email: books@capricornlink.com.au

ISBN-13: 978-1-4402-3213-8
SRN: V8199

Edited by **Stefanie Laufersweiler**
Desk edited by **Noel Rivera**
Designed by **Sarah Underhill**
Cover designed by **Sarah Underhill**
Steps photographed by **Kelly Wiese**
Location shots photographed by **Bangwallop**

Acknowledgments

I would like to thank Rachel Scheller for getting me through the proposal and initial stages of the book, and Ric Deliantoni for helping me improve my step-by-step photos. Many thanks also go to Stefanie Laufersweiler, my editor; she has been extremely patient and so easy to work with. Without beautiful seed beads and crystals, I couldn't come up with new designs, so my thanks also go to Betcey Ventrella from Beyond Beadery for always having such wonderful goodies to choose from. Finally, thanks to all of you who love romantic, delicate jewelry as much as I do. Without your support, this book wouldn't exist.

Dedication

This book is for:

My husband, Paul, who has given me his love and encouragement from day one, even on my crazy days—and believe me, there were a few of those.

My mom and dad, who are the most supportive parents a girl could have. They passed their creativity on to me, and for that I will be eternally grateful.

My good friend Virginia: She holds my hand on the airplane and is always there to encourage me when I am having doubts. She also reminds me when I need to put those big girl panties on.

These are the same wonderful people who supported me through my first book, and they stood by me again as this book became a reality. I love and thank you with all my heart. You mean the world to me!

Metric Conversion Chart

To convert	to	multiply by
Inches	Centimeters	2.54
Centimeters	Inches	0.4
Feet	Centimeters	30.5
Centimeters	Feet	0.03
Yards	Meters	0.9
Meters	Yards	1.1

Measurements have been given in imperial inches with metric conversions in parentheses. Use one or the other as they are not interchangeable. The most accurate results will be obtained using inches.

Desire more beading inspiration?
Then you'll love these other titles:

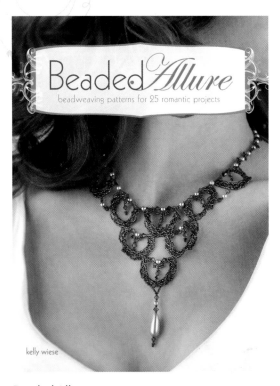

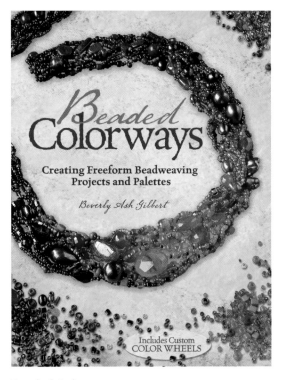

Beaded Allure
Beadweaving Patterns for 25 Romantic Projects
Kelly Wiese
Add a romantic twist to your creative time with *Beaded Allure*. Inside you'll find projects and techniques to give your beadweaving the soft and romantic aesthetic you've always dreamed of. Author Kelly Wiese will lead you through the ins and outs of a variety of stitches, and you'll use those stitches in 25 step-by-step projects.

Beaded Colorways
Creating Freeform Beadweaving Projects and Palettes
Beverly Ash Gilbert
Beaded Colorways offers beaders inspiration and direction for working with color and creating custom color mixes—which the author calls "bead soups"—based on colors in nature and other sources. Eighteen step-by-step projects exquisitely combine color work and beadweaving while incorporating a mix of materials.

Also visit
BeadingDaily.com

You'll find FREE projects, tutorials and e-books, blogs, reviews, special offers and more!

And join the fun at: @fwcraft

 facebook.com/fwcraft